MATT GROENING'S

THE SIMPSONS™
RAINY DAY
FUN BOOK

HarperPerennial
A Division of HarperCollins Publishers

TO THE MEMORY OF SNOWBALL I

YOU MAY BE GONE,
BUT YOUR MIDNIGHT YOWLING
STILL ECHOES IN OUR EARS.

THE SIMPSONS RAINY DAY FUN BOOK. Copyright ©1991 by Matt Groening Productions, Inc. All rights reserved. Printed in Hong Kong. No part of this book may be used or reproduced in any manner whatsoever without written permission except in the case of brief quotations embodied in critical articles and reviews. For information address HarperCollins Publishers, 10 East 53rd Street, New York, NY 10022.

ISBN 0-06-096861-3

RRD 10 9

Concepts, Design & Art Direction: Cindy Vance
Rainy Day Fun Team: Mary Trainor (Captain), Steve Vance, and Dyan Sheldon
Editor: Wendy Wolf
Design Associate: Peter Alexander
Production Assistant: Clare O'Callaghan
Illustration: Bill Morrison, John Adams, and Steve Vance
Production Director: Roz Barrow

THE SIMPSONS
RAINY DAY FUN BOOK

Introduction by Lisa Simpson

We Simpsons have long been devotees of mindless entertainment. So when the good folks at HarperCollins suggested we put together a Rainy Day Fun Book, our first reaction was "How useful! How productive! How boring!"

We'd seen these so-called fun books before -- scientific projects, mind-altering picture puzzles, educational card games. "Fun" indeed! Not for us these worthwhile pastimes. No way.

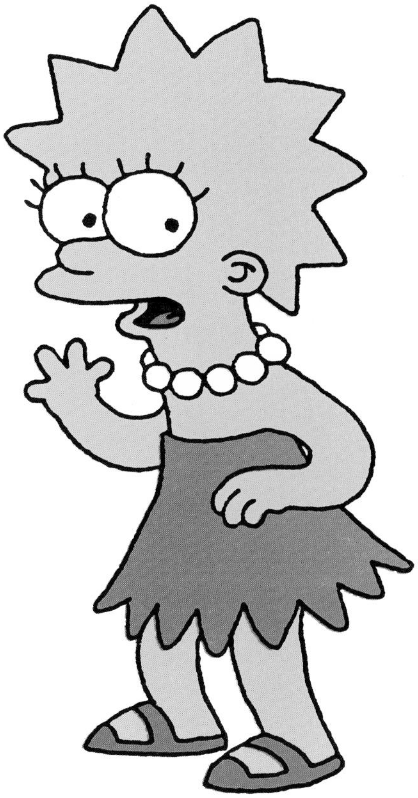
I WANTED A BOOK FRAUGHT WITH TENSION AND RIFE WITH PLOT!

What then, thought we, might be done to put the "F" back in fun? Why not create a new-age rainy day book with nothing whatsoever useful in it? Why not a book that's nearly as devoid of purpose as an evening of television? A book crammed with fun and fun by-products, with no redeeming educational value or significant political undercurrents. A SIMPSONS Rainy Day Fun Book.

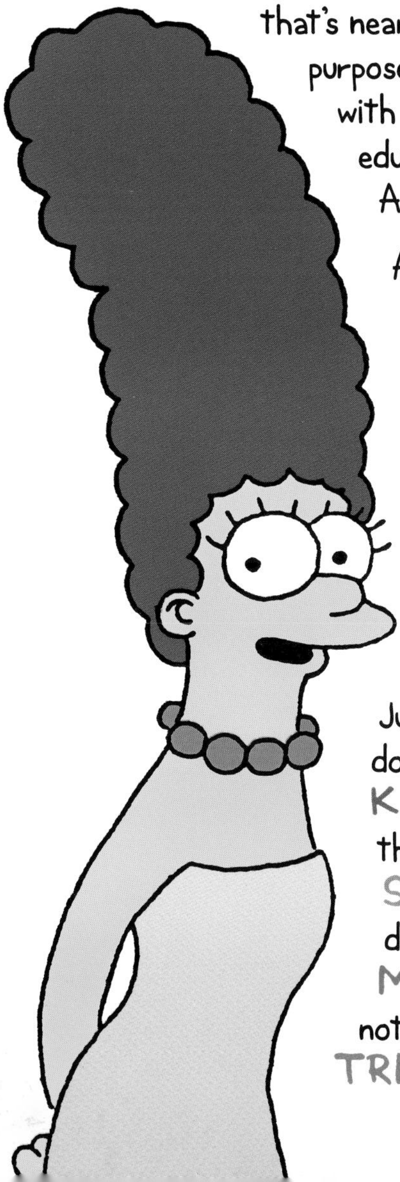
WELL, I FEEL IT SHOULD HAVE SOME EDUCATIONAL VALUE.

And here's what we've stuffed it full of: **PUT ON YOUR OWN TV SHOW**—Be your own Network Programmer! Write your own scripts! Cancel your own series! **GOOFY GOLF**—We haven't seen links this goofy since there was that explosion at the sausage factory! (Bart wrote that last joke.) **SECRET SPY TRICKS AND EYE TRICKS**—Lotsa top-secret stuff left over from the Cold War. Just reheat and serve. **GO NUTS FOR DONUTS**—Out there it's dog-eat-dog, but here at the Simpsons', just the reverse is true! **KRUSTY'S 3 RINGS-O-FUN**—We promise, not one dime from this book will go into that clown's pocket! **BART & LISA'S MAGIC SHOW**—The title tells all. **HOMER-DINI AGE-GUESSER**—Ta da! No age too awkward! Amazing, and not the least bit enlightening! **MAGGIE'S MIXED-UP PICTURE SCRAMBLE**—No, it's not much of a puzzle, but she's just a child, for goshsakes! **POINTLESS TRIVIA**—"Commit these to memory and you will enjoy lifelong popularity and social success!" claims my brother. You have been warned. Grampa's **ZOETROPE**—This thing is so old it's new! **PICNIC PANIC**—Yep. It's one of them pesky hidden picture puzzles. **ESCAPE FROM 4TH GRADE**—Join Bart for a casual stroll home from school. **ROAD TRIP**—Say WHAT?! Call the auto club, man . . . we're having a communication breakdown! **PENCIL PAGE**—Better put on your thinking caps for this one. Some clean socks wouldn't hurt, either. **LISA'S HOUSE O' MYSTERIES**—Prepare to be baffled, if not irked and peeved. **WHO SWIPED THE CUPCAKES?**—A chilling, real-life tale of greed and larceny . . . starring all your favorite Simpsons. **MADAME LISA'S MYSTICAL FORTUNE TELLER, WACKY TALKY TIN CANS, HUMAN SARDINES, ADMIRAL BART'S BATTLESHIP** and **WHO IS IT?**—A cornucopia of miscellaneous grab-bag surprises and tomfoolery. Too complicated to explain. **SIDESHOW BOB'S FLIPPED OUT FLIPBOOK**—An inside look at how a convicted felon passes his time behind bars. **SPITBALL DART BOARD**—The Sport of Kings. **MARGE'S WEEK-AT-A-GLANCE**—And you thought she was just a housewife! **OTTO'S WILD RIDE**—Fasten your seat belts, dudes. We're outta here! **HANDY SHADOW SHOWS, SILHOUETTES** and **SPINNING SPIRAL THINGY PAPER-MANIA**—A collection of basic paper tricks on which to build an entire repertoire of parlor games and stunts. Some real crowd-pleasers. **MESSIN' UP THE KITCHEN**—It was at this point in the book that we all got hungry and went into the kitchen for a bite to eat! **THE OFFICIAL HECK-OF-A-DECK SIMPSONS PLAYING CARDS**—Some of the all-time great card games of the Western world . . . and a deck of Simpsons' cards to play 'em with. **SOLUTIONS TO PUZZLES**—Why not do what Homer does? Start reading the book here!

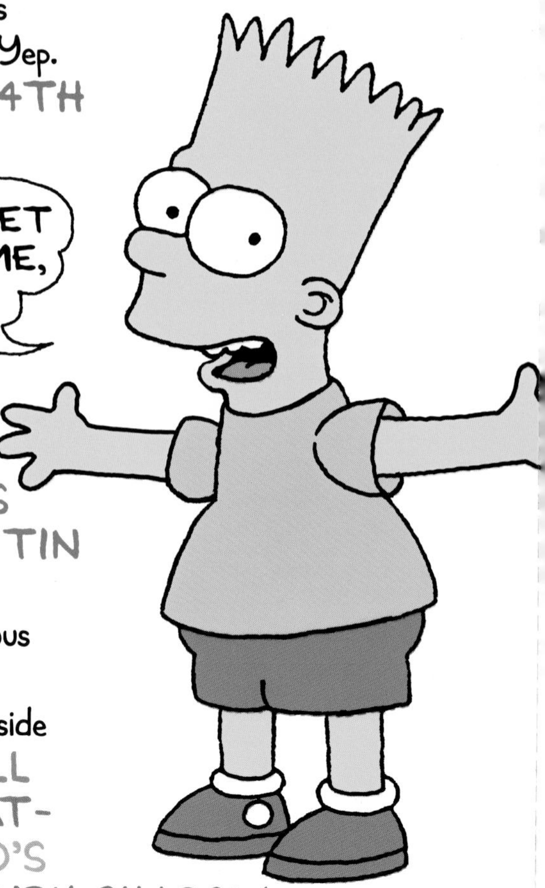
HELP! GET ME HOME, MAN!

Does all this sound too good to be true? You bet it is!

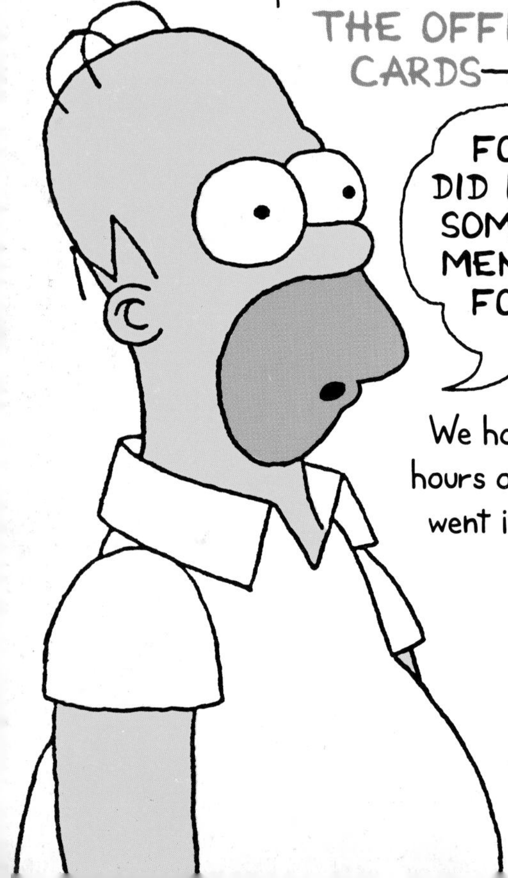
FOOD? DID I HEAR SOMEONE MENTION FOOD?

We hope this book will provide you with hours & hours of the same Simpson-style mental activity that went into creating it.

Have a Rainy Day!

Lisa Simpson

Lisa Simpson of
The Simpsons

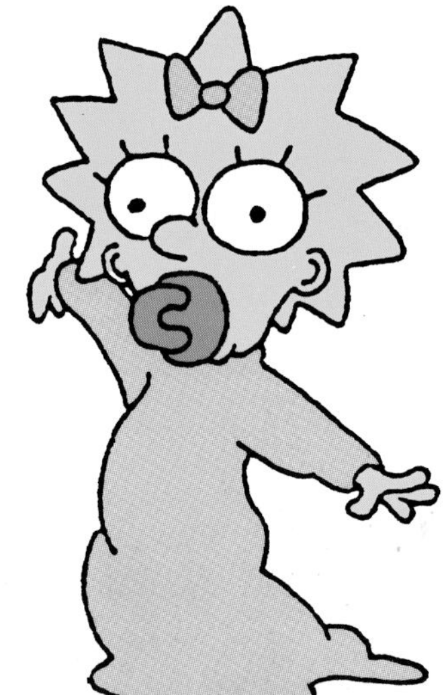

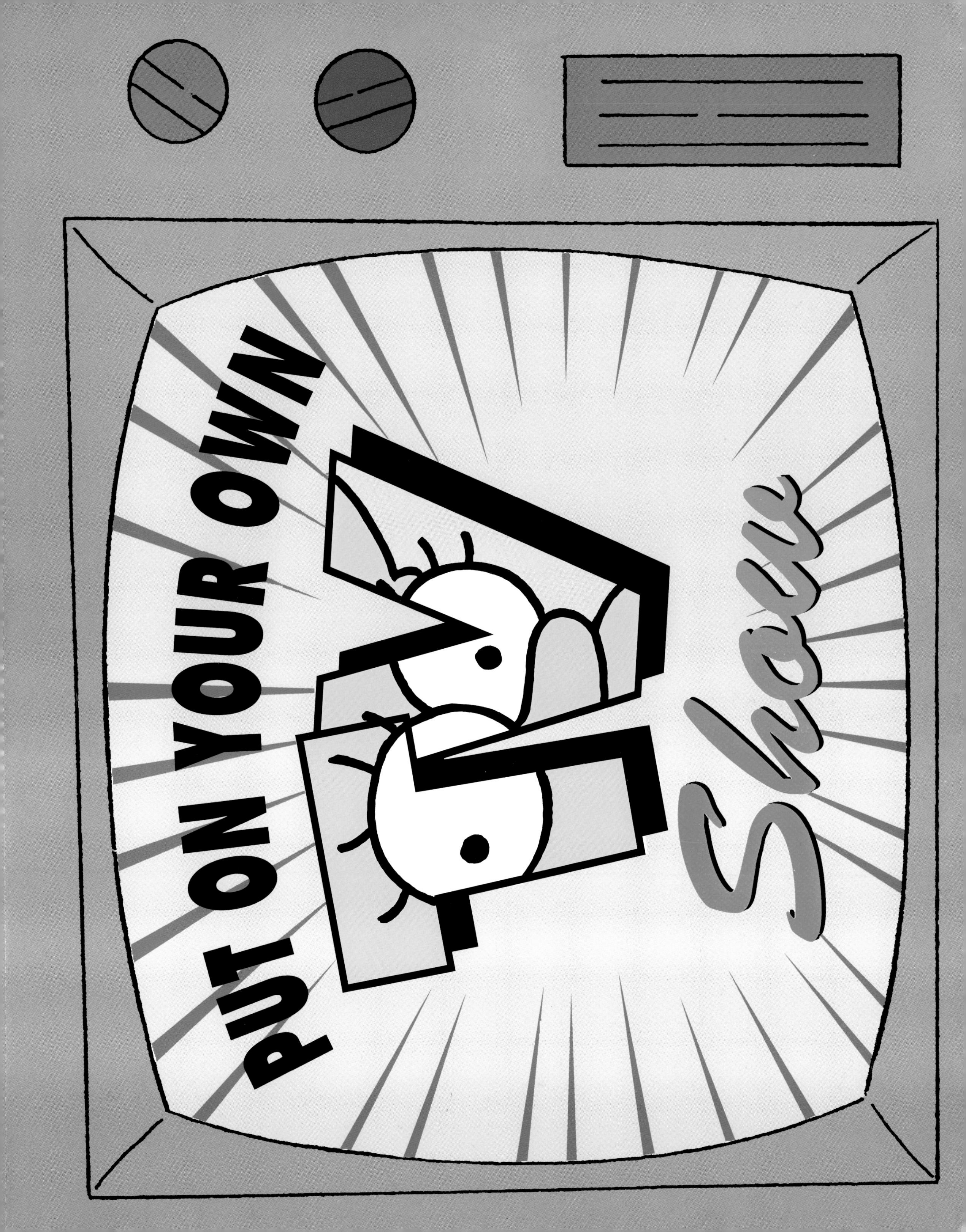
PUT ON YOUR OWN
TV
Show

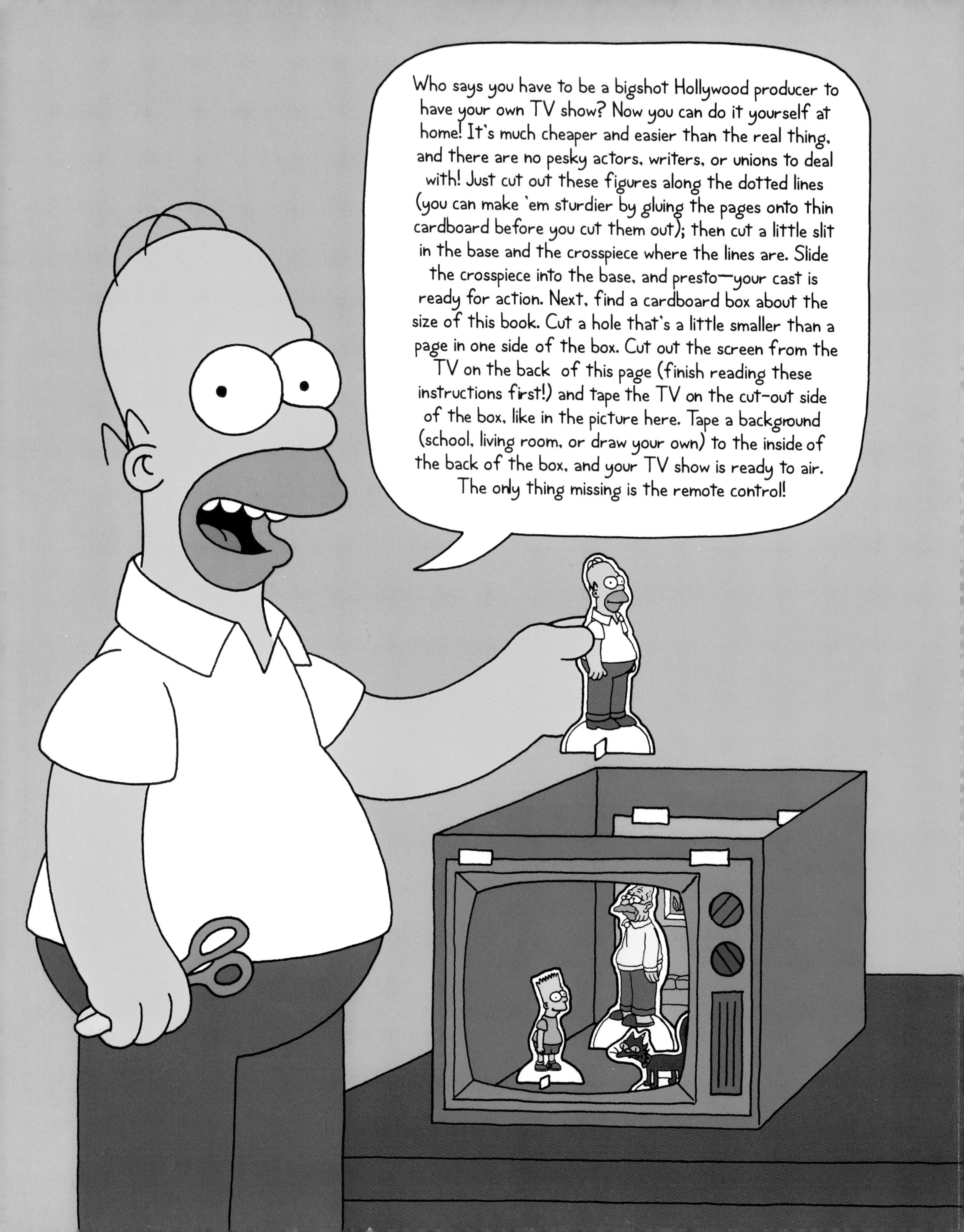
Who says you have to be a bigshot Hollywood producer to have your own TV show? Now you can do it yourself at home! It's much cheaper and easier than the real thing, and there are no pesky actors, writers, or unions to deal with! Just cut out these figures along the dotted lines (you can make 'em sturdier by gluing the pages onto thin cardboard before you cut them out); then cut a little slit in the base and the crosspiece where the lines are. Slide the crosspiece into the base, and presto—your cast is ready for action. Next, find a cardboard box about the size of this book. Cut a hole that's a little smaller than a page in one side of the box. Cut out the screen from the TV on the back of this page (finish reading these instructions first!) and tape the TV on the cut-out side of the box, like in the picture here. Tape a background (school, living room, or draw your own) to the inside of the back of the box, and your TV show is ready to air. The only thing missing is the remote control!

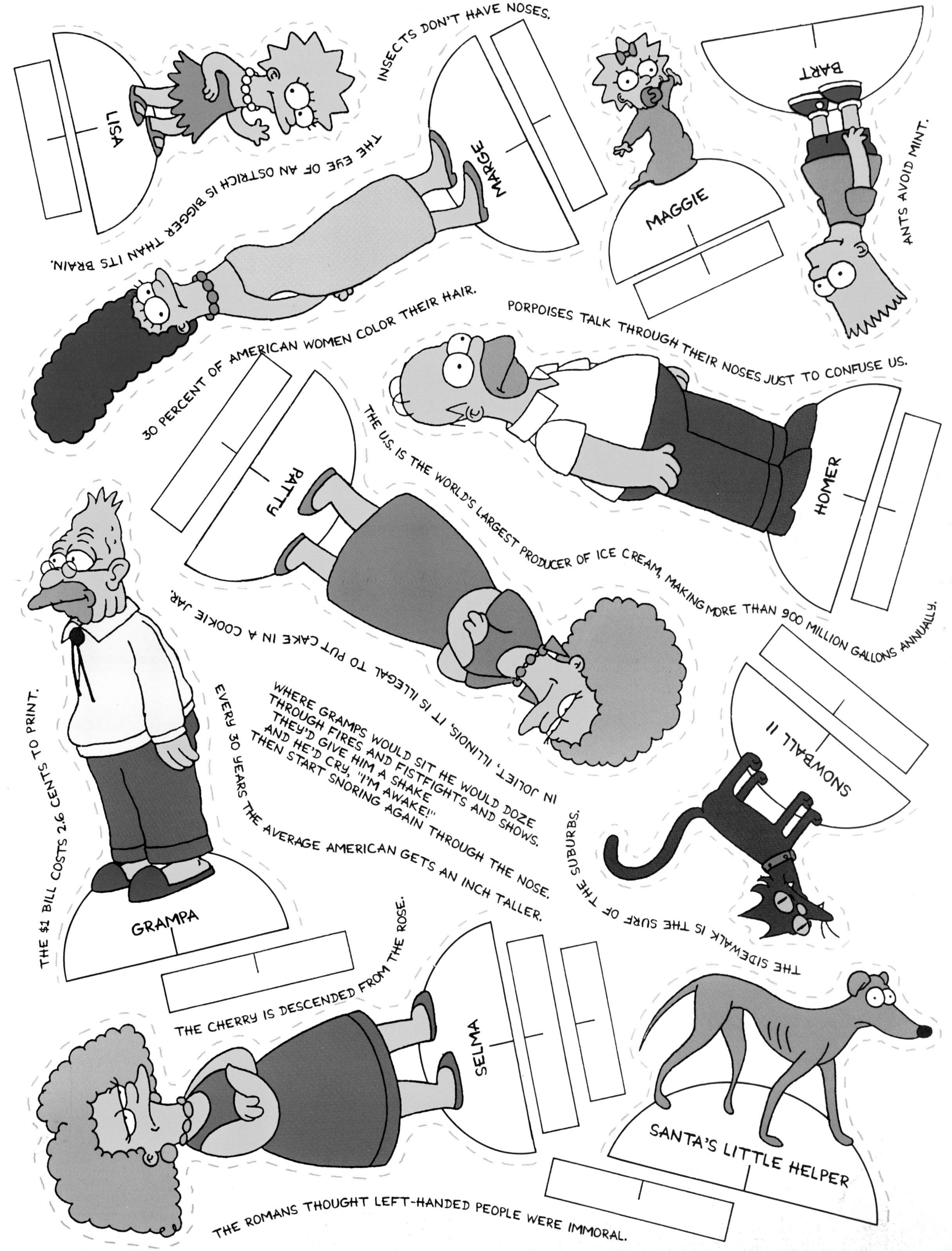

INSECTS DON'T HAVE NOSES.
LISA
MARGE
MAGGIE
BART
THE EYE OF AN OSTRICH IS BIGGER THAN ITS BRAIN.
ANTS AVOID MINT.
30 PERCENT OF AMERICAN WOMEN COLOR THEIR HAIR.
PORPOISES TALK THROUGH THEIR NOSES JUST TO CONFUSE US.
PATTY
HOMER
THE U.S. IS THE WORLD'S LARGEST PRODUCER OF ICE CREAM, MAKING MORE THAN 900 MILLION GALLONS ANNUALLY.
IN JOLIET, ILLINOIS, IT IS ILLEGAL TO PUT CAKE IN A COOKIE JAR.
WHERE GRAMPS WOULD SIT HE WOULD DOZE
THROUGH FIRES AND FISTFIGHTS AND SHOWS.
THEY'D GIVE HIM A SHAKE
AND HE'D CRY, "I'M AWAKE!"
THEN START SNORING AGAIN THROUGH THE NOSE.
EVERY 30 YEARS THE AVERAGE AMERICAN GETS AN INCH TALLER.
SNOWBALL II
THE $1 BILL COSTS 2.6 CENTS TO PRINT.
GRAMPA
THE SIDEWALK IS THE SURF OF THE SUBURBS.
THE CHERRY IS DESCENDED FROM THE ROSE.
SELMA
SANTA'S LITTLE HELPER
THE ROMANS THOUGHT LEFT-HANDED PEOPLE WERE IMMORAL.

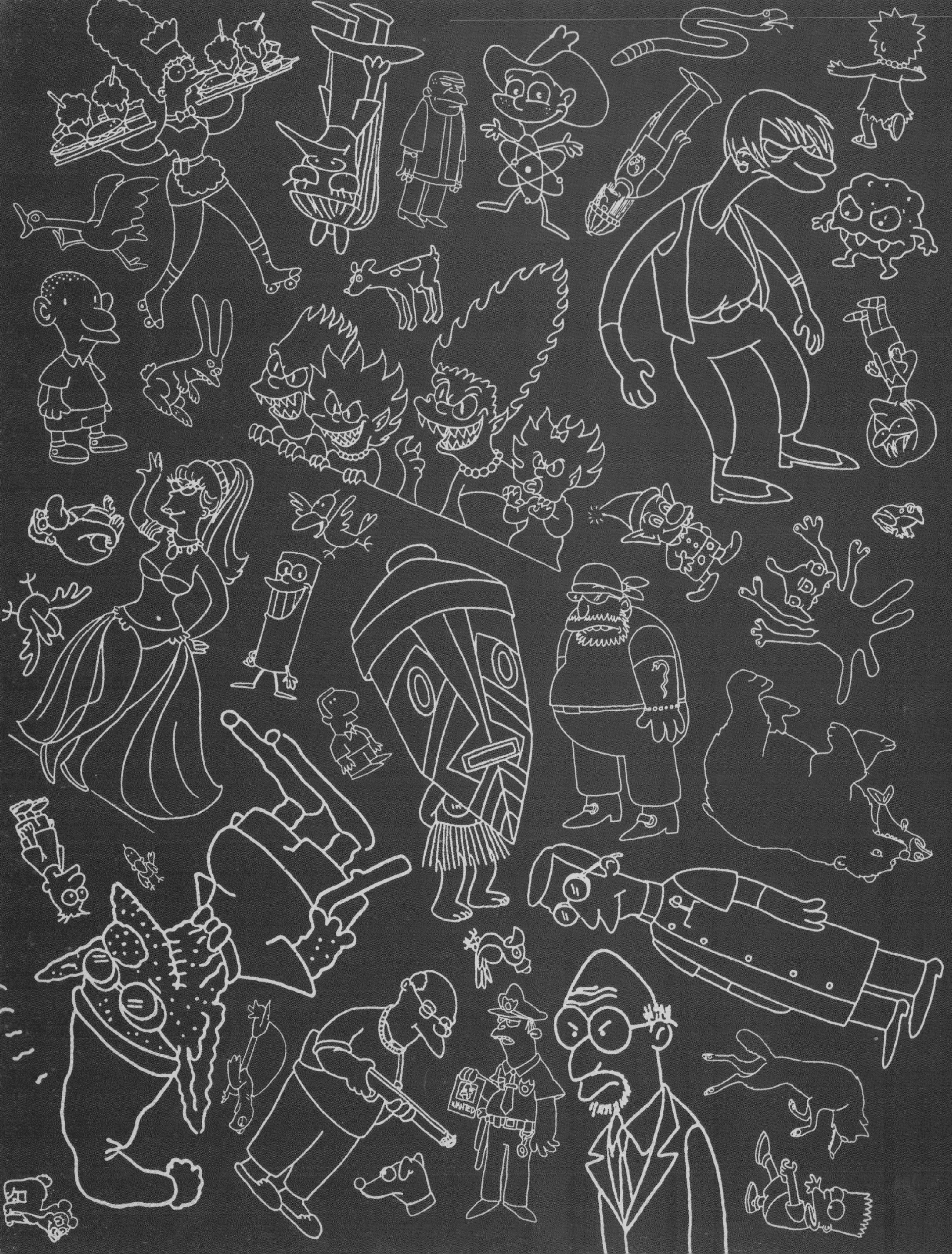
WANTED

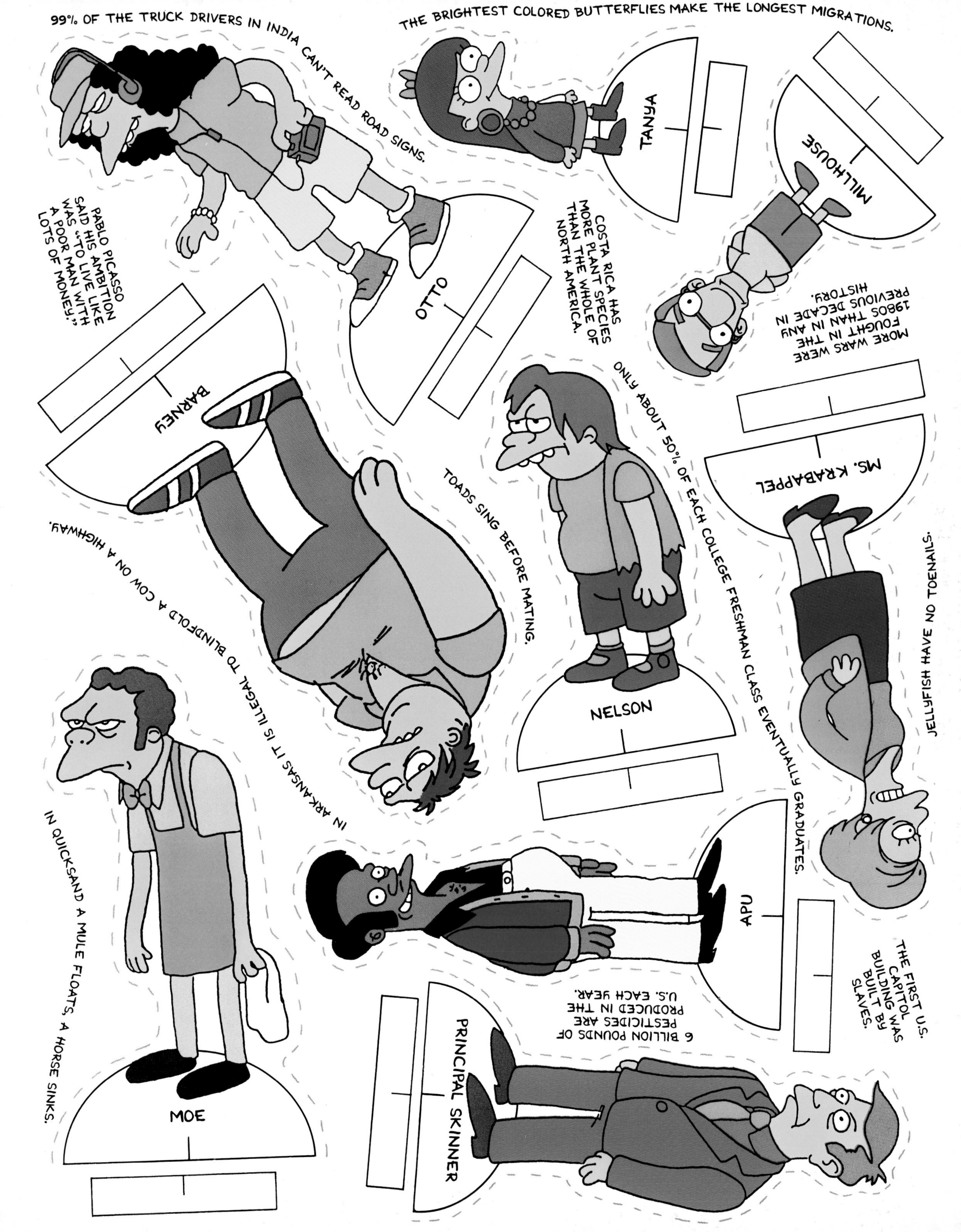
99% OF THE TRUCK DRIVERS IN INDIA CAN'T READ ROAD SIGNS.
THE BRIGHTEST COLORED BUTTERFLIES MAKE THE LONGEST MIGRATIONS.
TANYA
MILLHOUSE
PABLO PICASSO SAID HIS AMBITION WAS "TO LIVE LIKE A POOR MAN WITH LOTS OF MONEY."
COSTA RICA HAS MORE PLANT SPECIES THAN THE WHOLE OF NORTH AMERICA.
OTTO
MORE WARS WERE FOUGHT IN THE 1980S THAN IN ANY PREVIOUS DECADE IN HISTORY.
BARNEY
ONLY ABOUT 50% OF EACH COLLEGE FRESHMAN CLASS EVENTUALLY GRADUATES.
MS. KRABAPPEL
TOADS SING BEFORE MATING.
IN ARKANSAS IT IS ILLEGAL TO BLINDFOLD A COW ON A HIGHWAY.
JELLYFISH HAVE NO TOENAILS.
NELSON
APU
IN QUICKSAND A MULE FLOATS, A HORSE SINKS.
THE FIRST U.S. CAPITOL BUILDING WAS BUILT BY SLAVES.
6 BILLION POUNDS OF PESTICIDES ARE PRODUCED IN THE U.S. EACH YEAR.
PRINCIPAL SKINNER
MOE

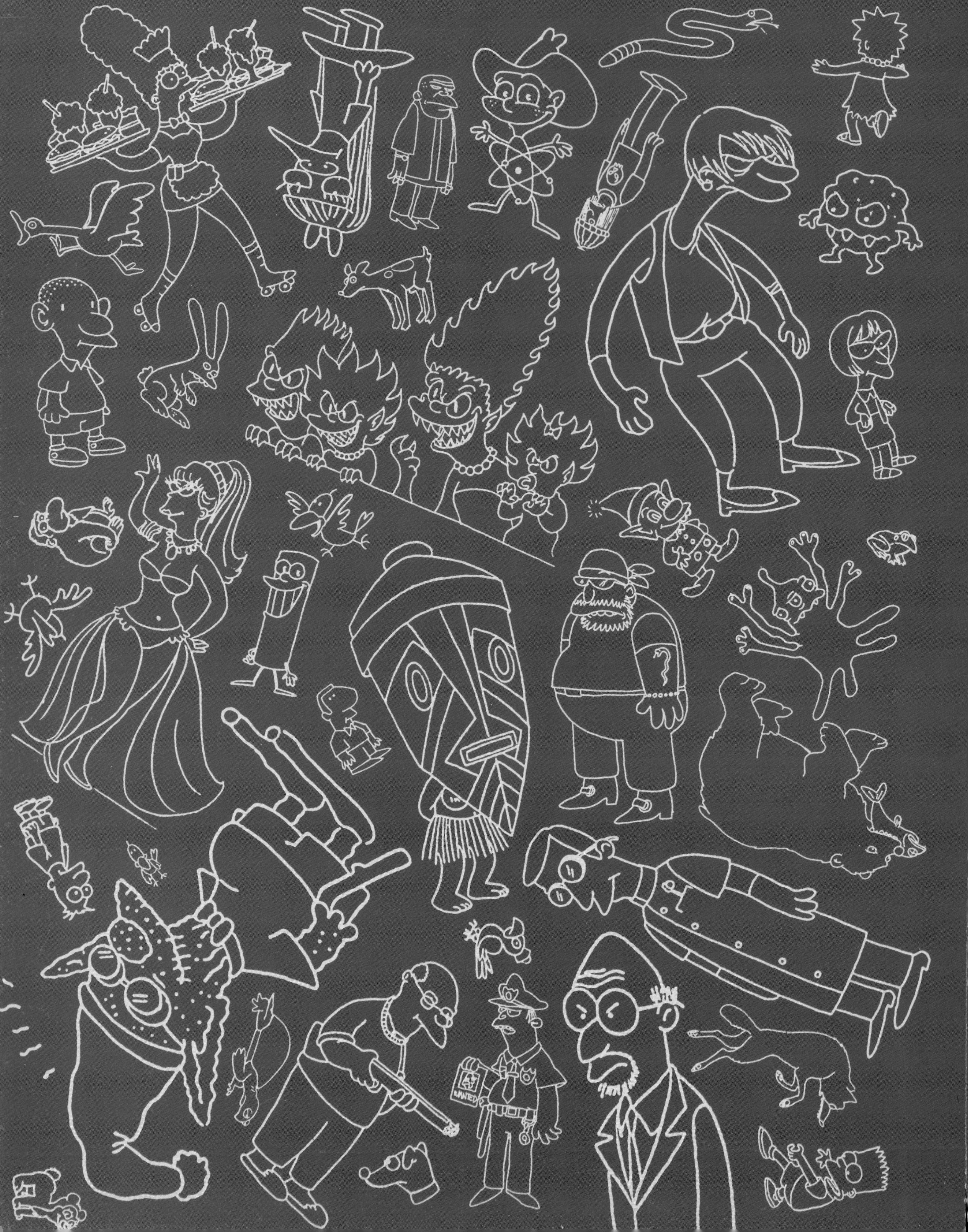
WANTED

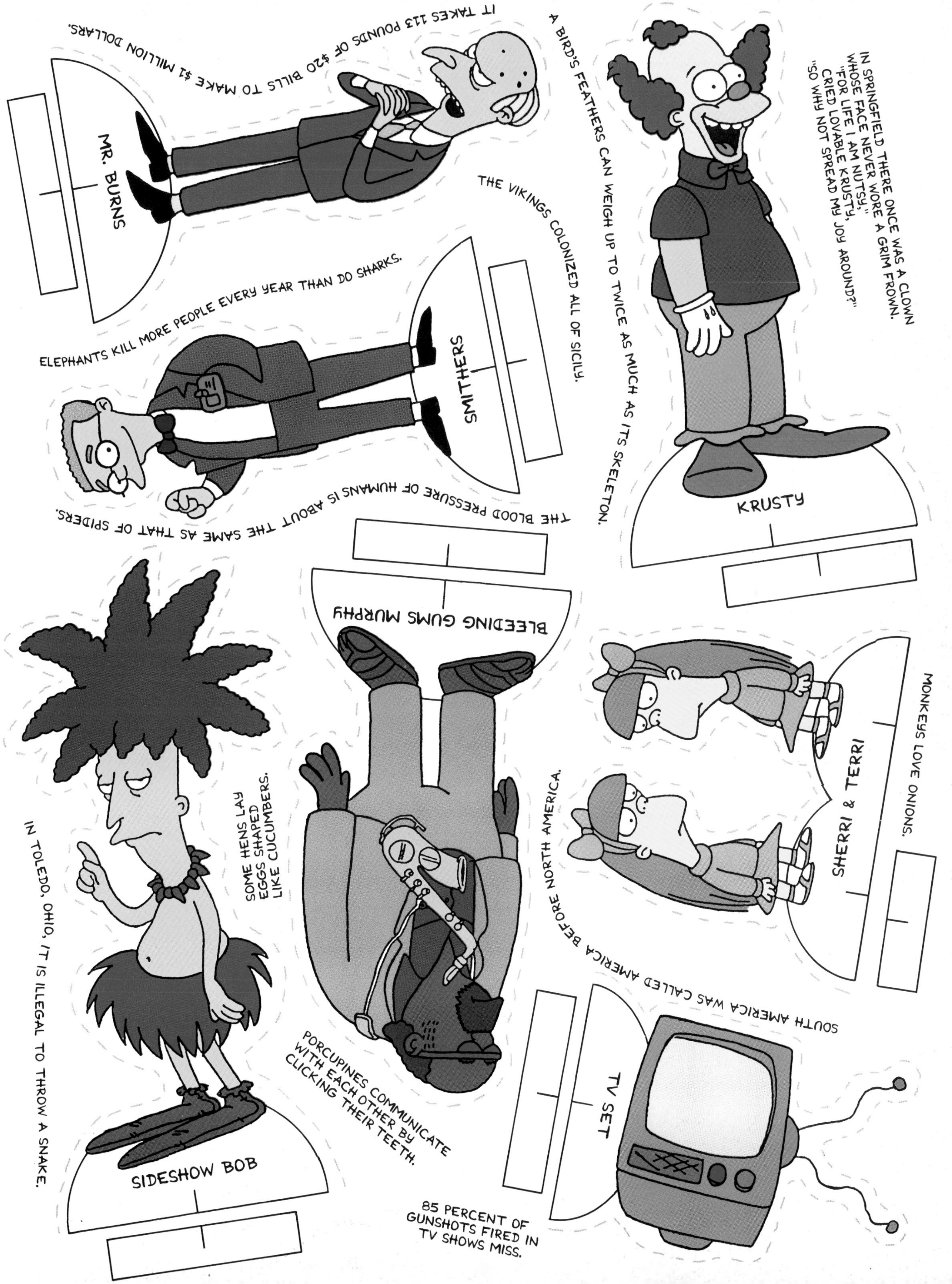
MR. BURNS
IT TAKES 113 POUNDS OF $20 BILLS TO MAKE $1 MILLION DOLLARS.
A BIRD'S FEATHERS CAN WEIGH UP TO TWICE AS MUCH AS ITS SKELETON.
IN SPRINGFIELD THERE ONCE WAS A CLOWN
WHOSE FACE NEVER WORE A GRIM FROWN.
"FOR LIFE I AM NUTSY,"
CRIED LOVABLE KRUSTY,
"SO WHY NOT SPREAD MY JOY AROUND?"
KRUSTY
THE VIKINGS COLONIZED ALL OF SICILY.
ELEPHANTS KILL MORE PEOPLE EVERY YEAR THAN DO SHARKS.
SMITHERS
THE BLOOD PRESSURE OF HUMANS IS ABOUT THE SAME AS THAT OF SPIDERS.
BLEEDING GUMS MURPHY
MONKEYS LOVE ONIONS.
SHERRI & TERRI
SOUTH AMERICA WAS CALLED AMERICA BEFORE NORTH AMERICA.
SOME HENS LAY
EGGS SHAPED
LIKE CUCUMBERS.
IN TOLEDO, OHIO, IT IS ILLEGAL TO THROW A SNAKE.
SIDESHOW BOB
PORCUPINES COMMUNICATE
WITH EACH OTHER BY
CLICKING THEIR TEETH.
TV SET
85 PERCENT OF
GUNSHOTS FIRED IN
TV SHOWS MISS.

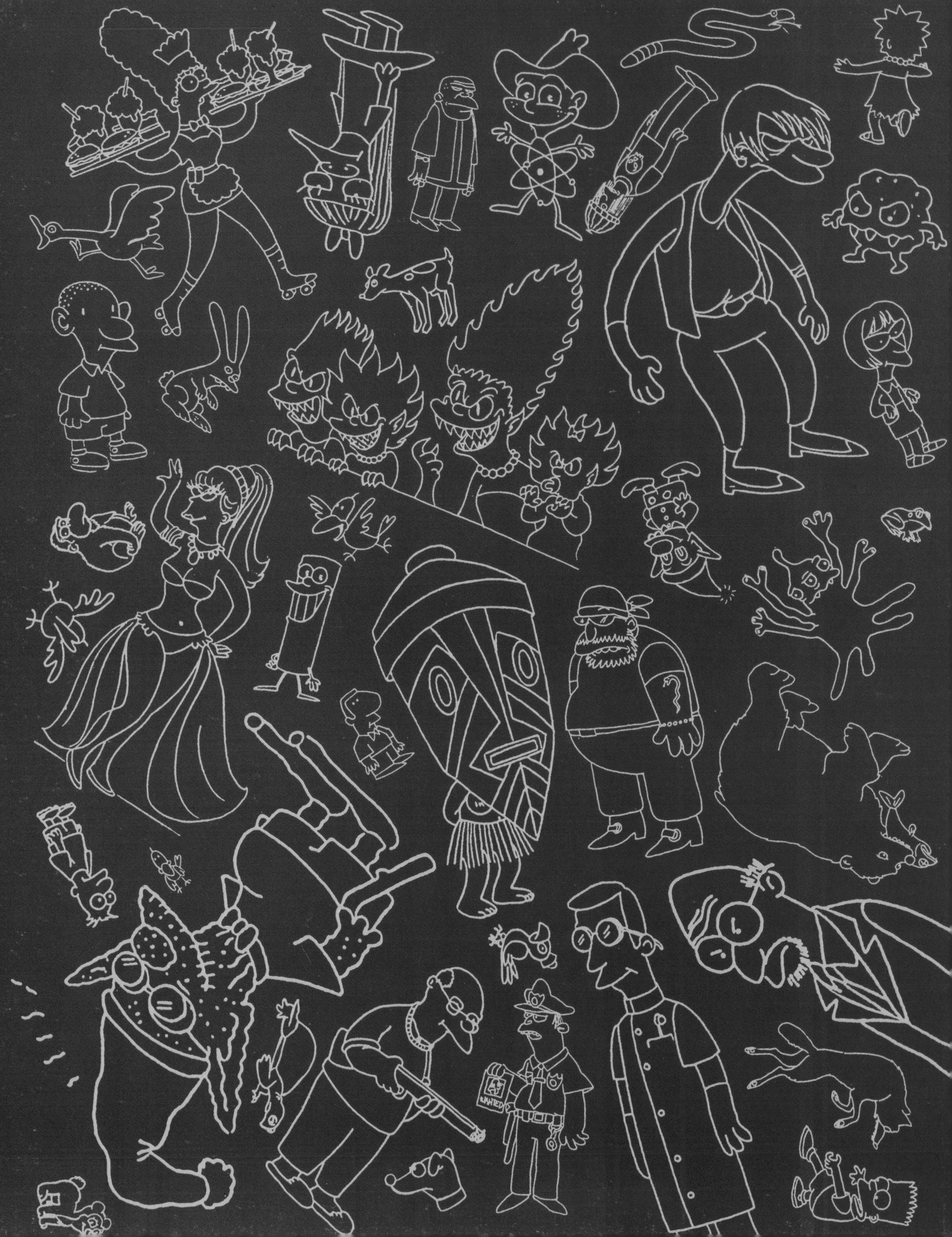
WANTED

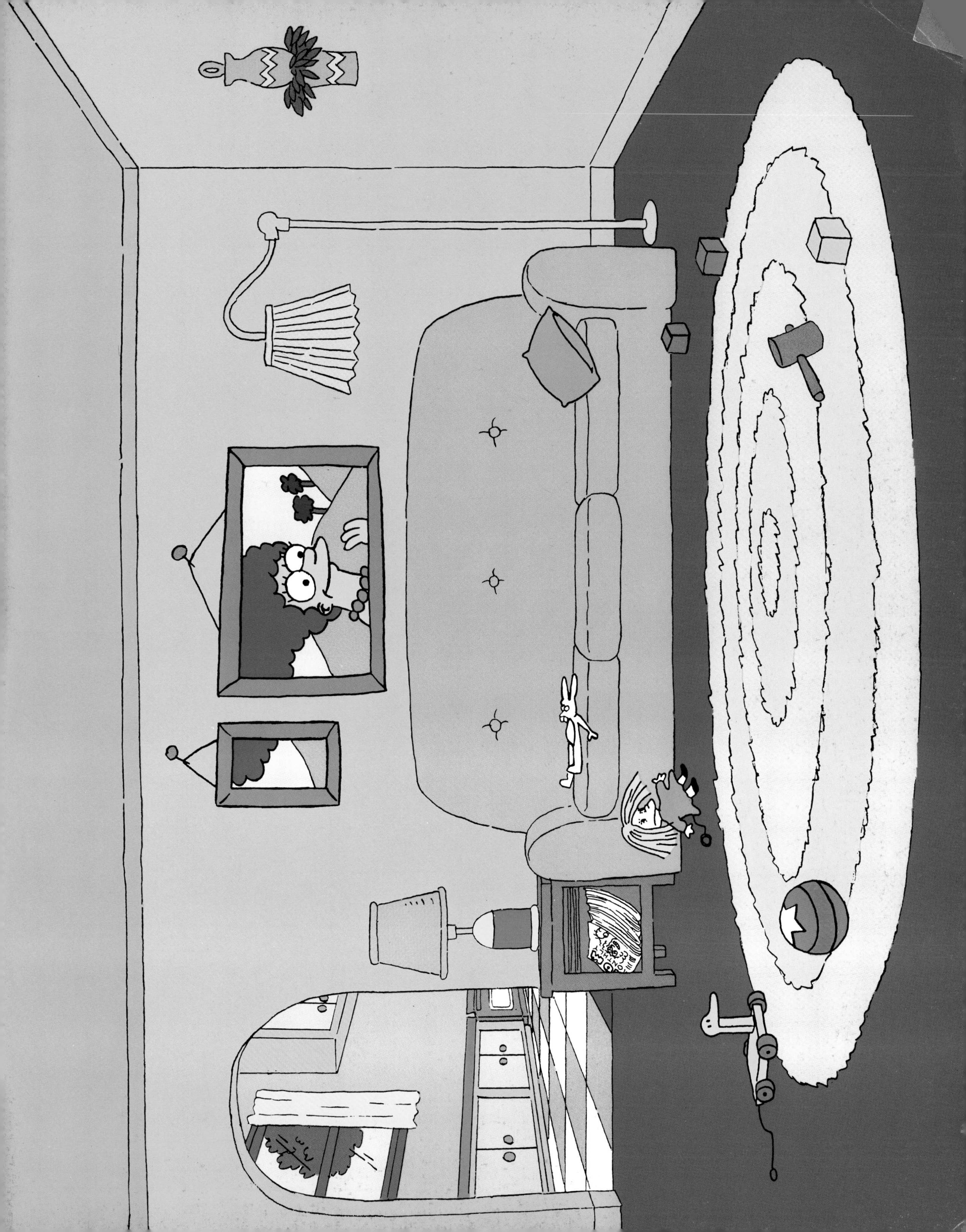

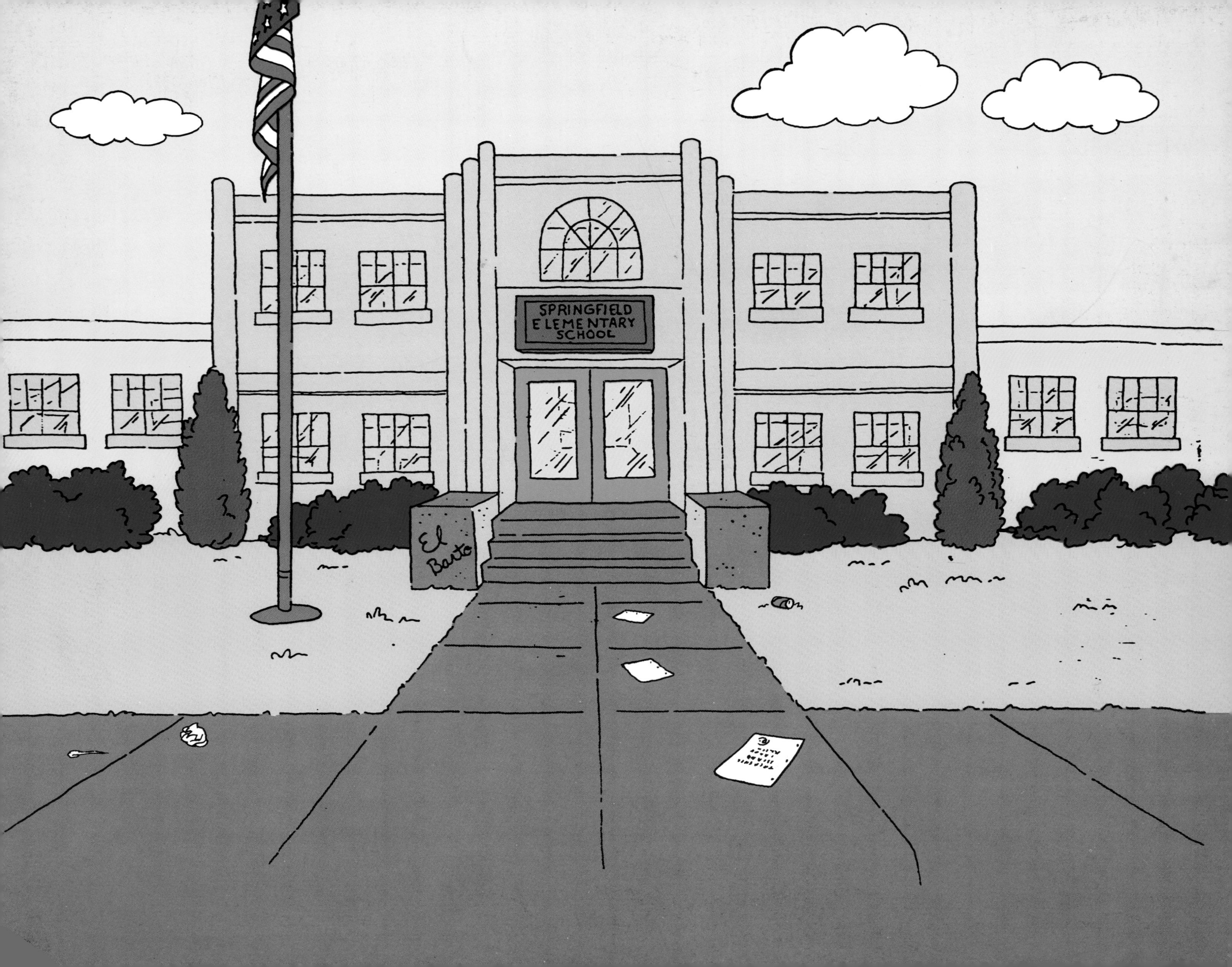
SPRINGFIELD
ELEMENTARY
SCHOOL
El Barto

The Simpsons' Goofy Golf

YOU CAN SET THIS GAME UP INSIDE OR OUT, DEPENDING ON THE WEATHER. MAKE THE COURSE AS COMPLICATED AS POSSIBLE. USE STICKS, BROOMS, BASEBALL BATS OR SOMETHING SIMILAR AS THE PUTTER. PING-PONG BALLS OR WADDED-UP ALUMINUM FOIL WORKS WELL INSIDE. USE A REGULAR BALL OUTSIDE.

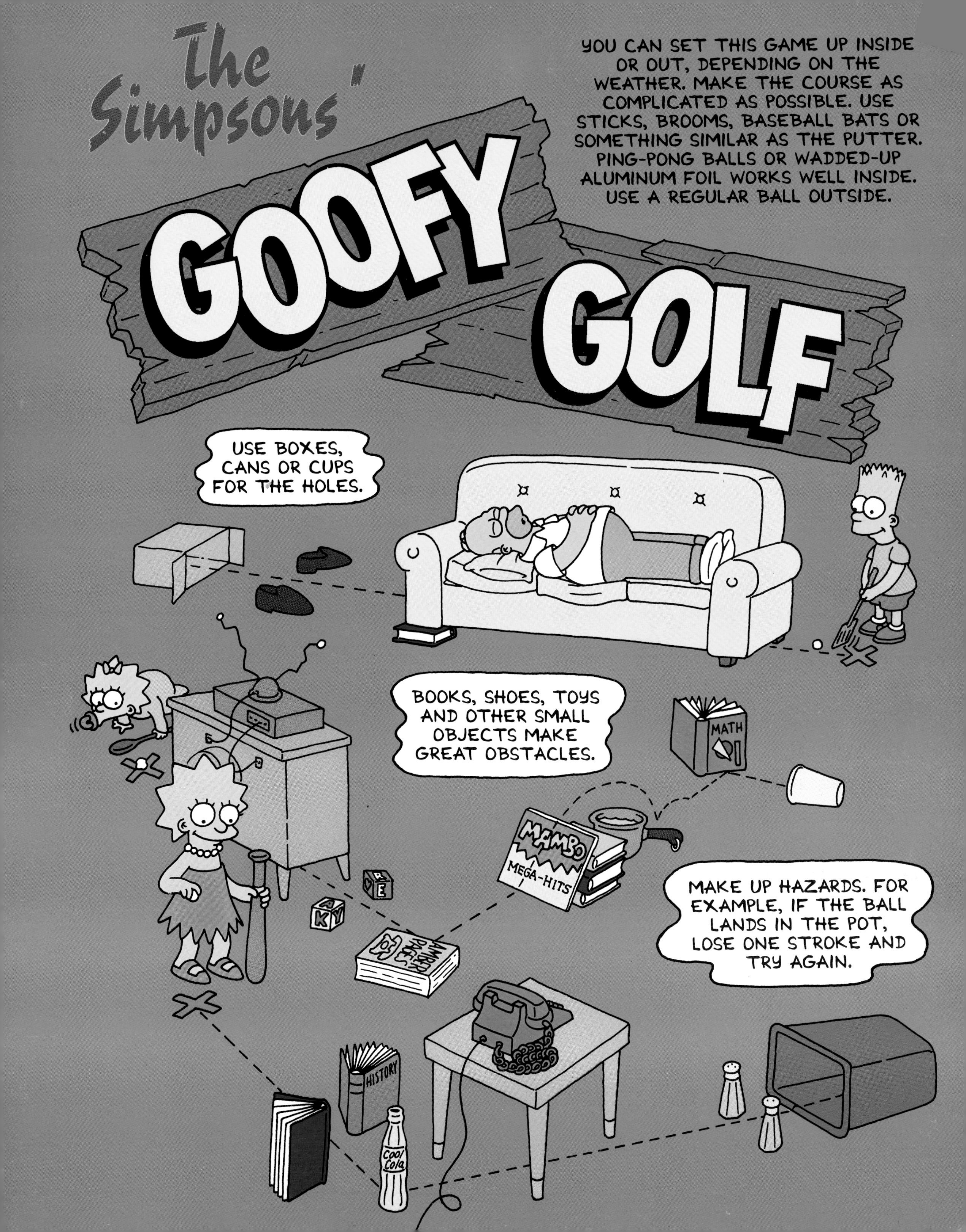
USE BOXES, CANS OR CUPS FOR THE HOLES.
BOOKS, SHOES, TOYS AND OTHER SMALL OBJECTS MAKE GREAT OBSTACLES.
MATH
MAMBO MEGA-HITS
MAKE UP HAZARDS. FOR EXAMPLE, IF THE BALL LANDS IN THE POT, LOSE ONE STROKE AND TRY AGAIN.
AMBER PAGES
HISTORY
Cool Cola

SECRET SPY TRICKS

GIVE THESE OPTICAL ILLUSIONS A TRY. YOU MIGHT BE SURPRISED BY THE ANSWERS!

A
B
C
D

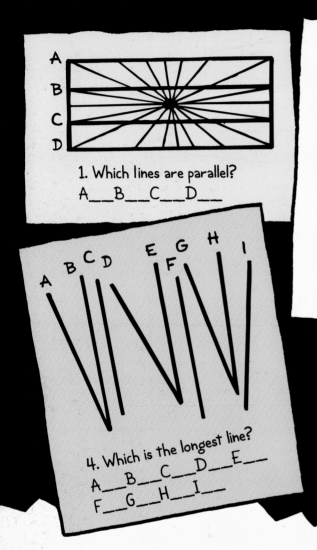

1. Which lines are parallel?
A___B___C___D___

A
B
C

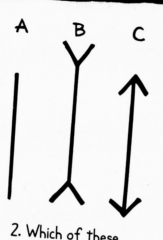

2. Which of these lines is the longest?
A___B___C___

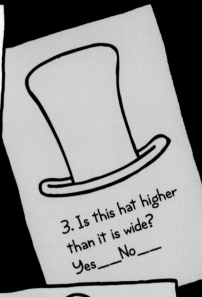

3. Is this hat higher than it is wide?
Yes___No___

A B C D E F G H I

4. Which is the longest line?
A___B___C___D___E___
F___G___H___I___

A
B

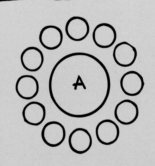

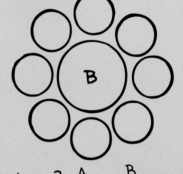

5. Which inner circle is the larger? A____B____

Answers on Page 64.

HANDY HAND ALPHABET

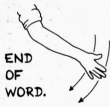

END OF WORD.

END OF SENTENCE.

USE THE HAND SIGNALS BELOW TO SEND SECRET MESSAGES TO A FRIEND WHO ALSO KNOWS THEM. WHEN YOU'RE AT THE END OF A WORD, MOVE YOUR HAND BACK AND FORTH WITH YOUR PALM FACE DOWN. DO THE SAME THING WITH BOTH HANDS TO SIGNAL THE END OF A SENTENCE. TRY USING SHORTHAND FOR SOME LETTERS LIKE A "C" FOR THE WORD "SEE" OR A "U" FOR THE WORD "YOU."

INVISIBLE INK

You can use milk, lemon juice or vinegar for ink. Or you can make a solution of 1/2 cup water and 1/2 cup sugar or salt. Use a matchstick, brush or cotton swab as a pen. Write on regular paper and let it dry. Your correspondent can read the message by pressing the paper with a slightly warm iron or putting it near a lighted electric bulb.

A
B
C
D
E
F
G
H
I
J
K
L
M

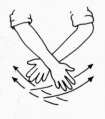

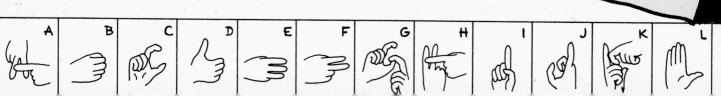

AND EYE TRICKS

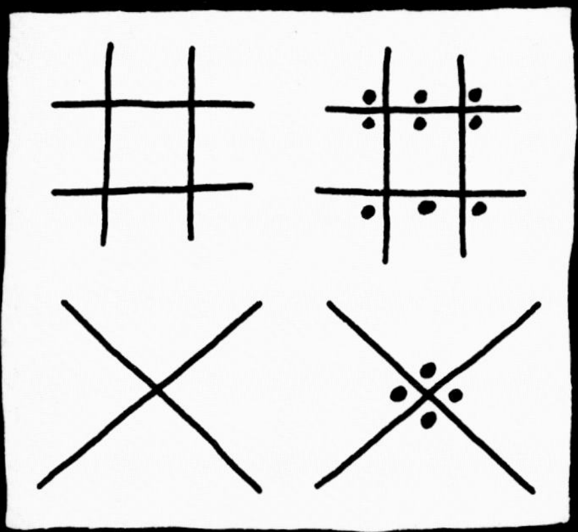

FIRST DRAW THESE LINES AND DOTS AS SHOWN HERE.

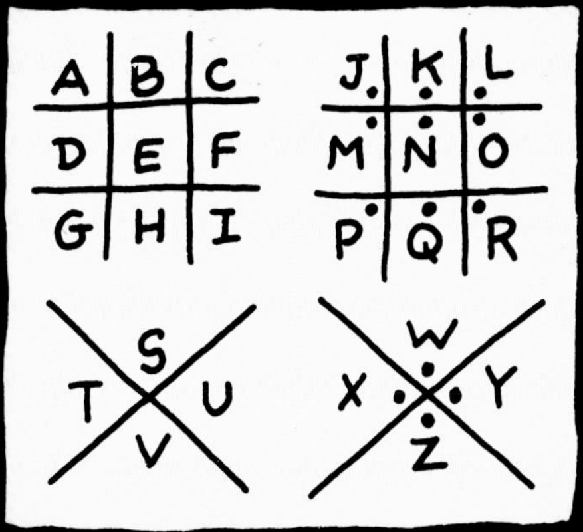
A B C
D E F
G H I
J K L
M N O
P Q R
S T U V
W X Y Z

NOW WRITE IN THE LETTERS OF THE ALPHABET LIKE THIS.

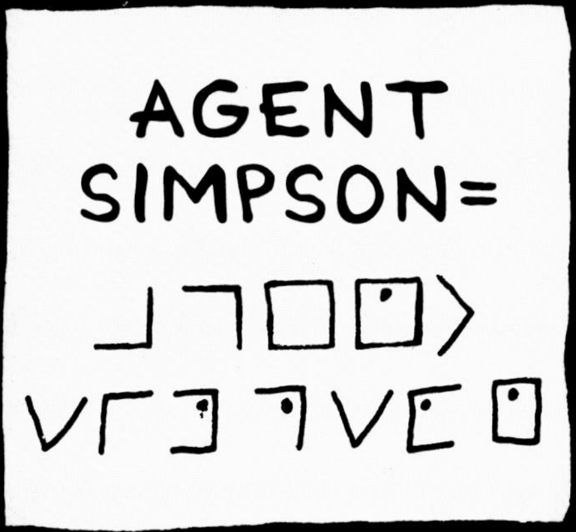
AGENT SIMPSON=

USE THE LINES OR LINES AND DOTS TO STAND FOR EACH LETTER.

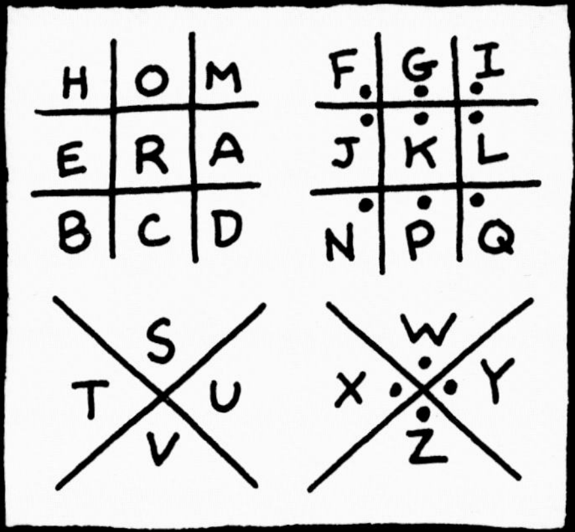
H O M
E R A
B C D
F G I
J K L
N P Q
S T U V
W X Y Z

TO MAKE IT MORE COMPLEX, START WITH A KEY WORD AND THEN ADD THE REST OF THE ALPHABET.

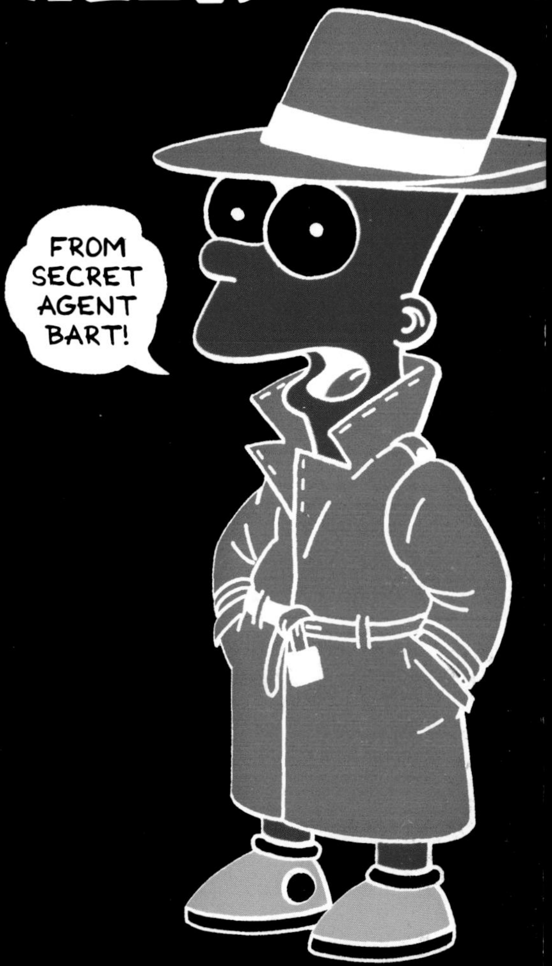
FROM SECRET AGENT BART!

STARE AT THIS PICTURE FOR 30 SECONDS, THEN STARE AT A BLANK WHITE WALL.

CUT OUT A SMALL SQUARE OF GRAY PAPER AND PUT IT AGAINST A PIECE OF RED OR GREEN PAPER. COVER BOTH WITH A TISSUE AND STARE AT THE SQUARE. IT WILL LOOK EITHER BLUE-GREEN OR RED, DEPENDING ON THE BACKGROUND.

TAKE A REGULAR PENCIL. HOLD IT LOOSELY AT ONE END BETWEEN YOUR THUMB AND FOREFINGER AND SHAKE IT UP AND DOWN. THE PENCIL WILL LOOK LIKE IT'S MADE OF RUBBER!

TRICKY TRANSFER WRITING

GET SOME PAPER REALLY WET AND LAY IT ON A HARD SURFACE. PUT A DRY PIECE OF PAPER OVER IT AND WRITE YOUR SECRET MESSAGE, PRESSING DOWN FIRMLY. THE MESSAGE WILL APPEAR ON THE WET PAPER WHEN YOU HOLD IT UP TO A LIGHT. IT WILL DISAPPEAR WHEN IT'S DRY. YOUR FRIEND CAN BRUSH IT WITH WATERY INK OR PAINT TO MAKE IT PERMANENT.

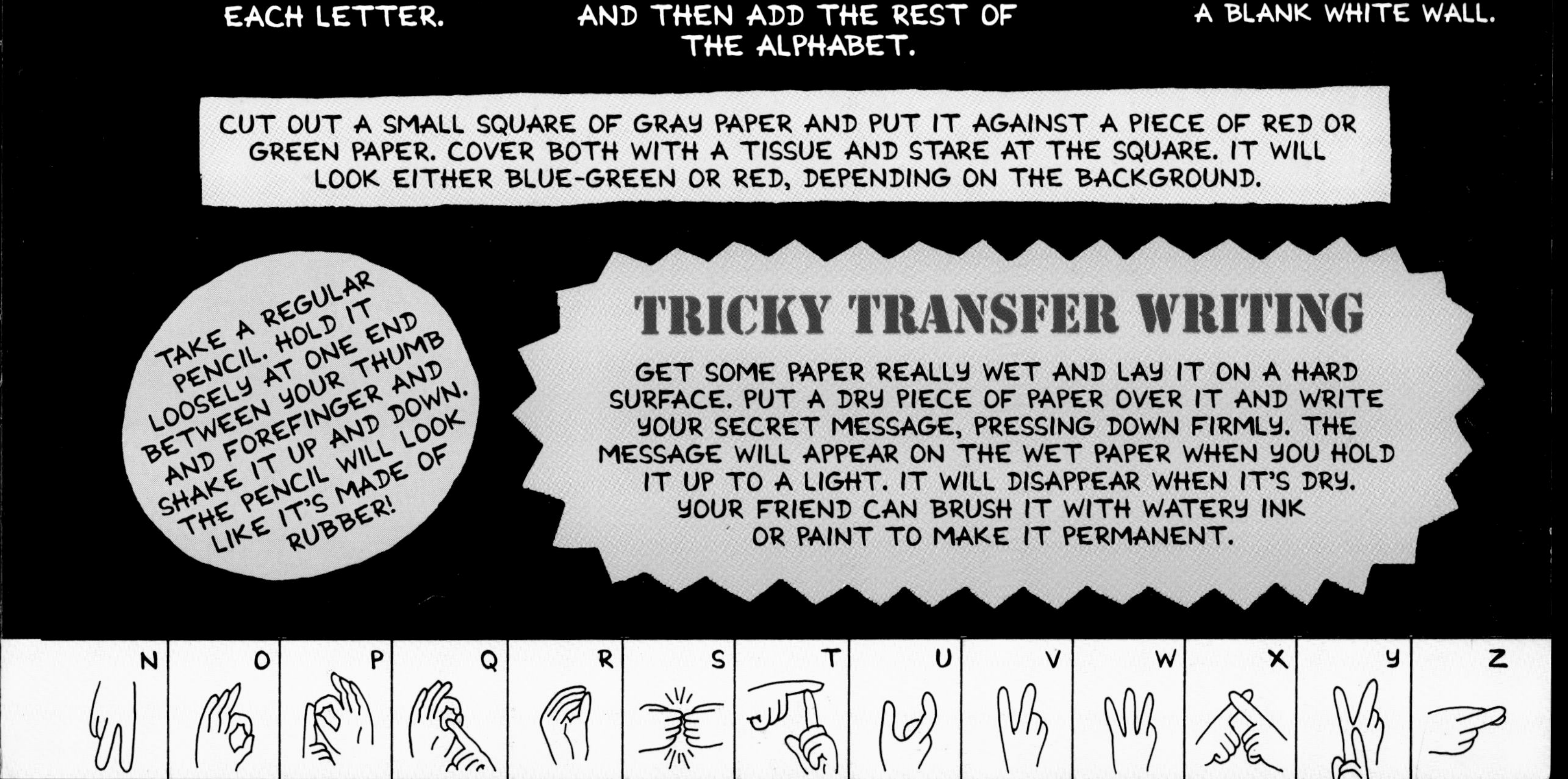
N O P Q R S T U V W X Y Z

THE SIMPSONS

GO NUTS FOR DONUTS

Marge has just returned from The Donut Hut with a box of scrumptious, gooey donuts. Only one path leads to the center. Who will get the donuts?

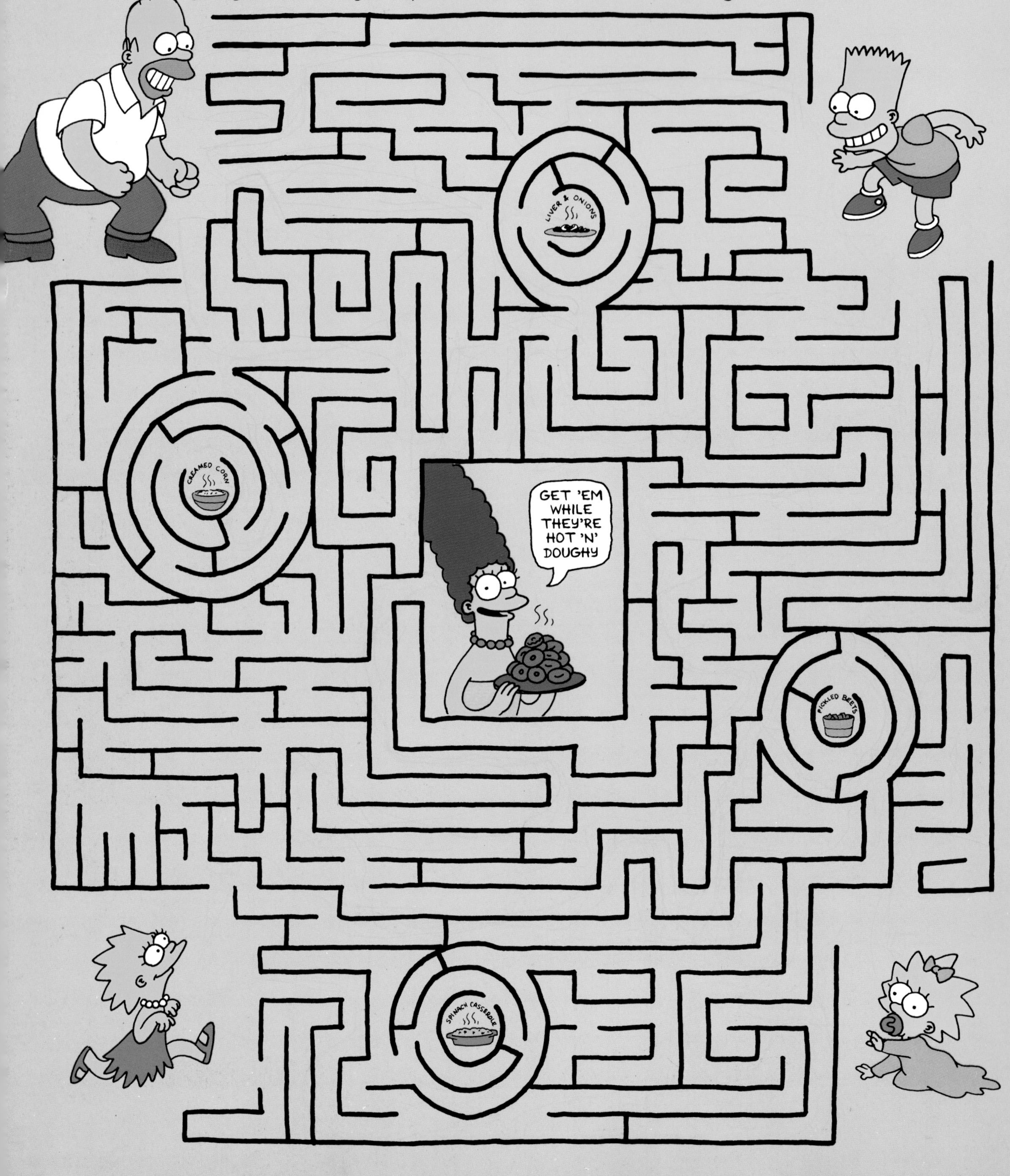

LIVER & ONIONS
CREAMED CORN
GET 'EM WHILE THEY'RE HOT 'N' DOUGHY
PICKLED BEETS
SPINACH CASSEROLE

SOLUTION ON PAGE 62.

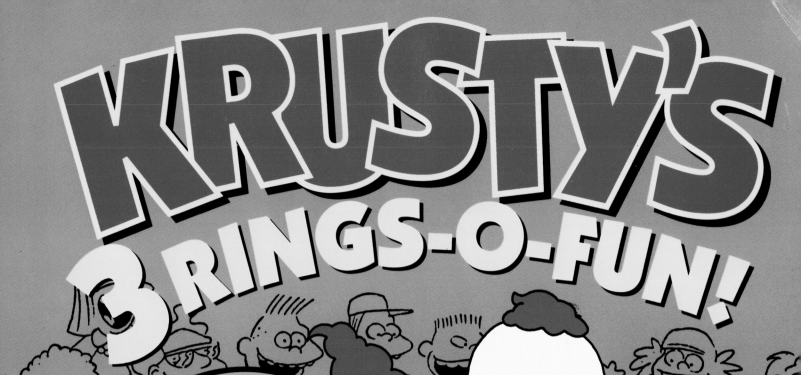

KRUSTY'S 3 RINGS-O-FUN!

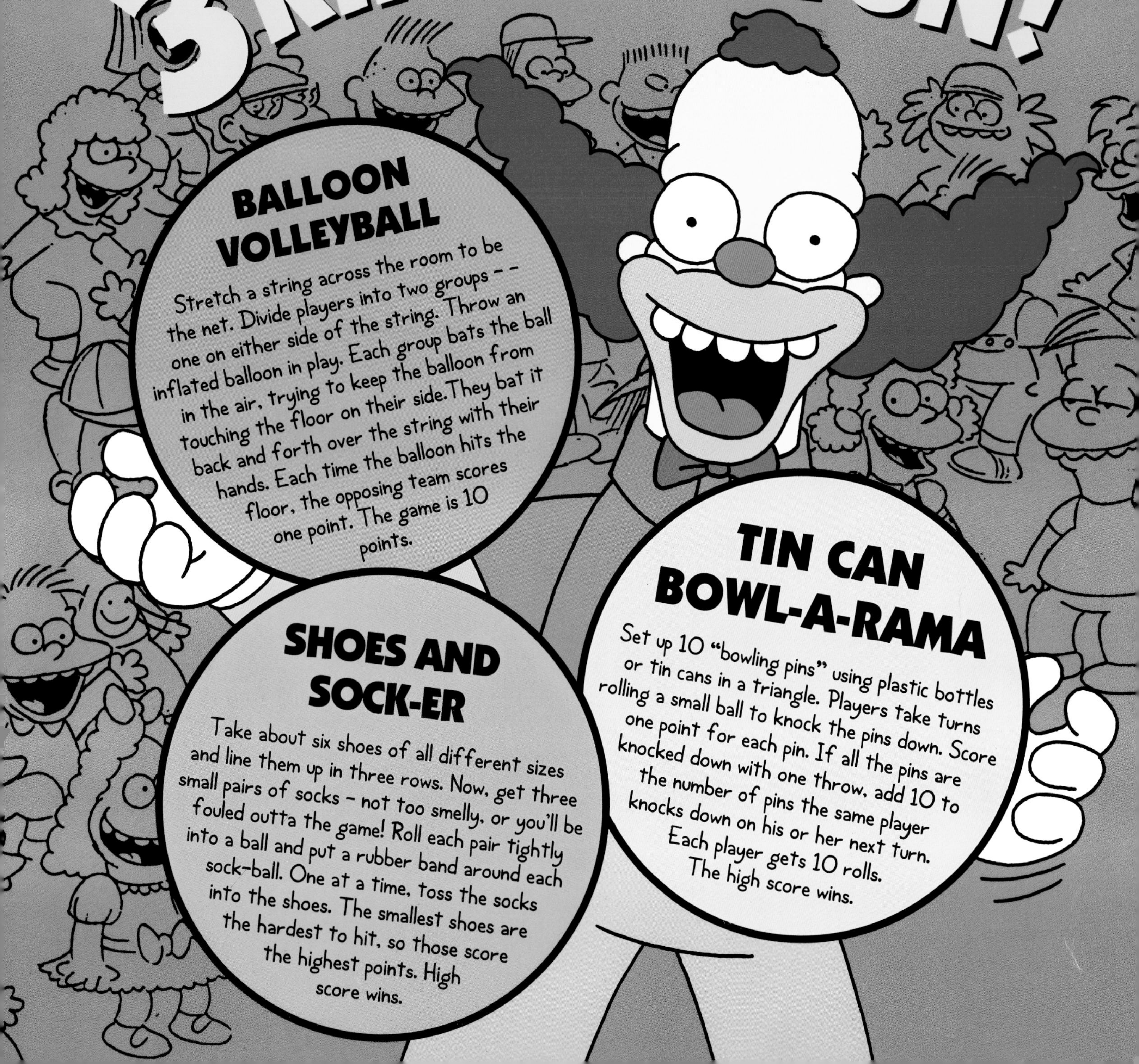

BALLOON VOLLEYBALL

Stretch a string across the room to be the net. Divide players into two groups -- one on either side of the string. Throw an inflated balloon in play. Each group bats the balloon in the air, trying to keep the balloon from touching the floor on their side. They bat it back and forth over the string with their hands. Each time the balloon hits the floor, the opposing team scores one point. The game is 10 points.

SHOES AND SOCK-ER

Take about six shoes of all different sizes and line them up in three rows. Now, get three small pairs of socks – not too smelly, or you'll be fouled outta the game! Roll each pair tightly into a ball and put a rubber band around each sock-ball. One at a time, toss the socks into the shoes. The smallest shoes are the hardest to hit, so those score the highest points. High score wins.

TIN CAN BOWL-A-RAMA

Set up 10 "bowling pins" using plastic bottles or tin cans in a triangle. Players take turns rolling a small ball to knock the pins down. Score one point for each pin. If all the pins are knocked down with one throw, add 10 to the number of pins the same player knocks down on his or her next turn. Each player gets 10 rolls. The high score wins.

OH NO! YOU'VE BROKEN EVERY BONE IN YOUR NOSE!

PLACE YOUR PALMS TOGETHER, FINGERS POINTING UP, AND GRIP YOUR NOSE BETWEEN YOUR TWO FOREFINGERS. PUT THE THUMBNAIL OF YOUR RIGHT HAND BEHIND YOUR UPPER FRONT TEETH. TWIST YOUR NOSE TO ONE SIDE WITH YOUR FOREFINGERS AND, AT THE SAME TIME, CLICK YOUR THUMBNAIL ON YOUR TEETH BY PRESSING YOUR THUMB FORWARD.

BART & LISA'S Magic Show

Mesmerizing X-RAY HAND

Roll a piece of paper into a thin tube and hold it up to one eye while keeping both eyes open. Hold it with one hand and place your other hand with the palm facing you, so that the side of the hand is touching the tube. Remember to keep both eyes open. As you look through the tube, move your hand toward you and away from you until you can see a hole in the middle of your hand.

Mystical MELDING GLASSES

USE TWO GLASSES THAT ARE THE SAME SIZE. PUT A CANDLE IN THE BOTTOM GLASS. LIGHT IT AND PLACE A THICK PIECE OF WET PAPER OVER IT. NOW PUT THE OTHER GLASS ON TOP AS SHOWN. THE CANDLE WILL GO OUT AND THE GLASSES WILL BE STUCK TOGETHER. TO TAKE APART, RUN UNDER HOT WATER.

ADULT SUPERVISION REQUIRED!

Confusing FUSING STRINGS

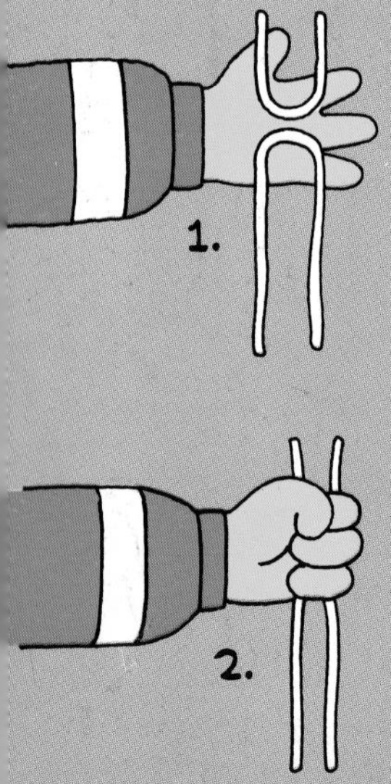

USE ONE LONG AND ONE SHORT STRING. FOLD THEM BOTH IN HALF AND HOLD THEM IN YOUR HAND AS IN ILLUSTRATION #1. CLOSE YOUR HAND TO SHOW. IT WILL LOOK LIKE PICTURE #2. PUT THE STRINGS IN YOUR POCKET WITH THE LONG ENDS HANGING OUT. PULL THE STRING BY ONE END. THE SHORT PIECE STAYS IN YOUR POCKET.

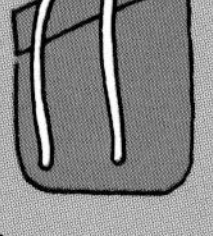

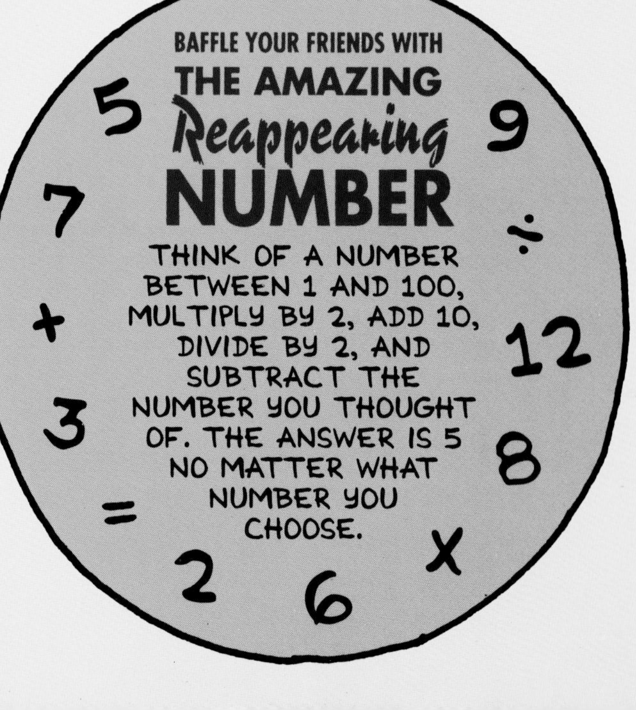

1.
2.
3.

4.

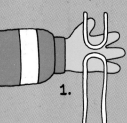

BAFFLE YOUR FRIENDS WITH THE AMAZING Reappearing NUMBER

THINK OF A NUMBER BETWEEN 1 AND 100, MULTIPLY BY 2, ADD 10, DIVIDE BY 2, AND SUBTRACT THE NUMBER YOU THOUGHT OF. THE ANSWER IS 5 NO MATTER WHAT NUMBER YOU CHOOSE.

5 9
7 ÷
+ 12
3 8
= X
2 6

Self-Inflating MIRACLE BALLOON

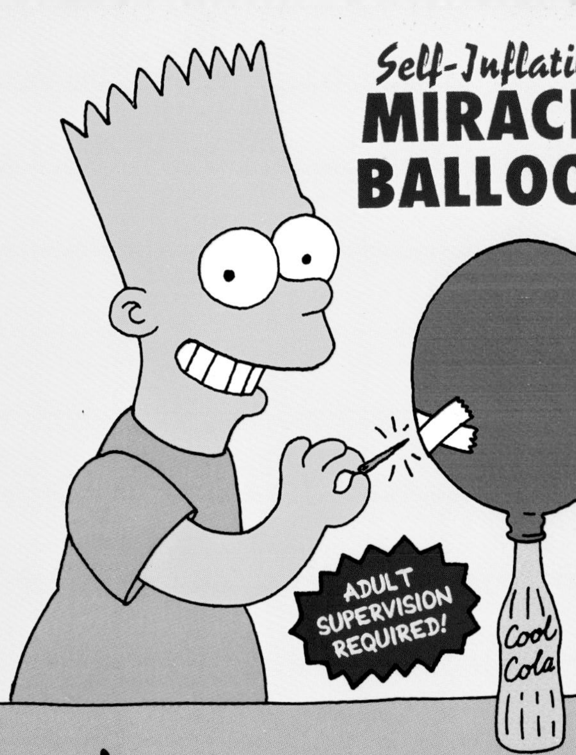
ADULT SUPERVISION REQUIRED!
Cool Cola

IF YOU PUT A LITTLE VINEGAR INTO A BOTTLE WITH A NARROW NECK, ADD A SMALL BIT OF BAKING SODA AND QUICKLY PLACE A BALLOON OVER THE OPENING, IT WILL BLOW UP THE BALLOON.

NOW TAKE THAT BALLOON (OR BLOW ONE UP) AND TIE IT TIGHTLY. PUT A PIECE OF CLEAR TAPE ON THE BALLOON. NOW YOU CAN POKE A REGULAR STRAIGHT PIN THROUGH THE TAPE WITHOUT BURSTING THE BALLOON!

Blackjack Bart's ALL-TIME BEST CARD TRICK

Deal 21 cards face up in 3 piles of 7 cards each. Ask someone to select mentally one of the cards and to think about it. When the 3 piles are dealt, ask him which pile his card is in. Now gather up the piles but be sure to put the pile containing the selected card in the middle of the stack. Deal again and ask which pile the card is in. Put this pile in the center of the stack, between the other two piles. Deal the cards a third time. When the person tells you which pile his card is in you pick out the card for him. The chosen card will be the fourth from the bottom of the pile indicated after the third deal. This never fails.

Extraordinary EGG-SUCKING BOTTLE

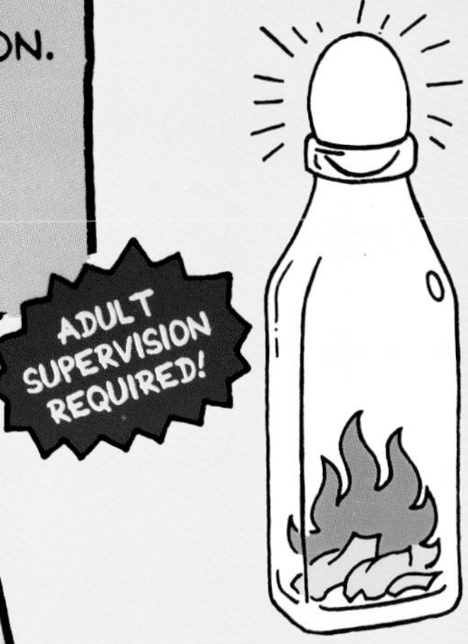
ADULT SUPERVISION REQUIRED!

Take an empty bottle with a neck slightly smaller than an egg's width. Hardboil an egg and peel it. Place a few pieces of paper inside the bottle and light them with a match. As they burn, place the egg on top of the bottle and see egg-zactly what happens!

To read this mysterious message, hold the book flat just below your eye level and view from the bottom of the page.

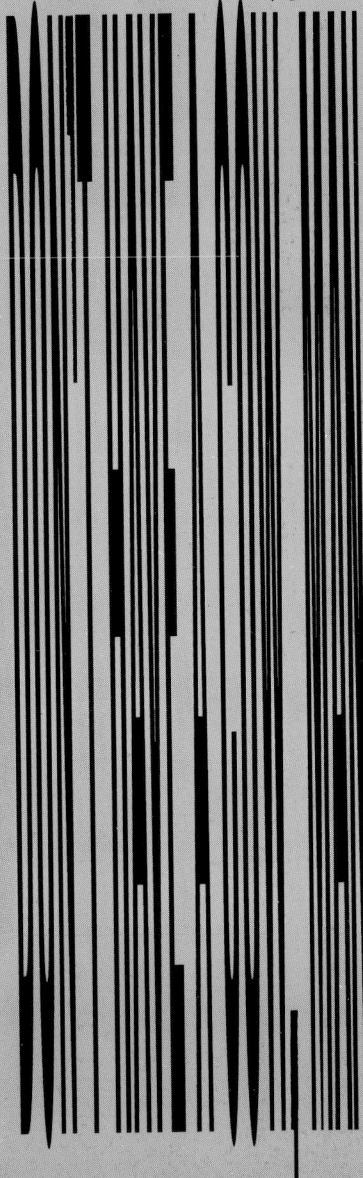

The Great Salt & Pepper Swindle

Fill a clear saltshaker most of the way with salt. Place a paper napkin over the top of the shaker. Push it down a little and fill with pepper. Screw the top back onto the shaker. Tear off the extra napkin. Now shake out some "salt" and amaze your friends!

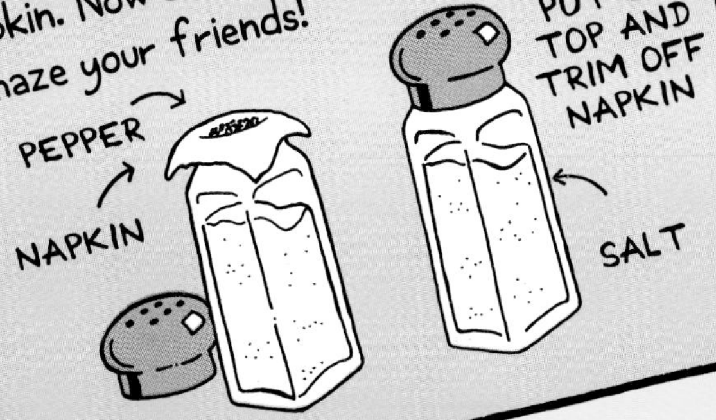
PEPPER
NAPKIN
PUT ON TOP AND TRIM OFF NAPKIN
SALT

THE GREAT HOMER-DINI

KNOWS ALL · SEES ALL · TELLS ALL · EATS ALL

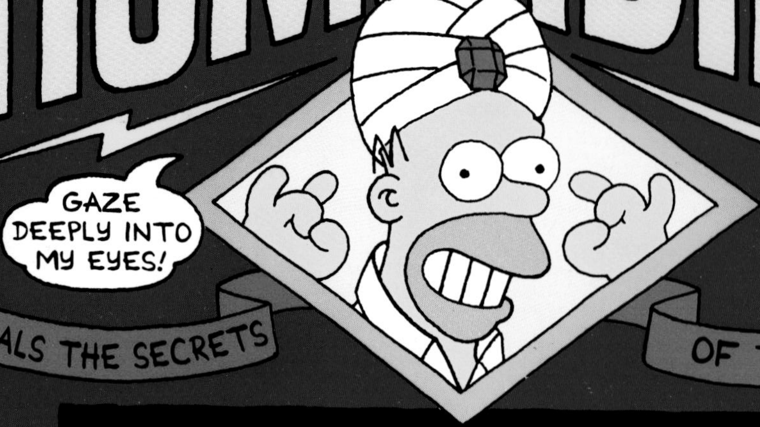
GAZE DEEPLY INTO MY EYES!

REVEALS THE SECRETS OF THE AGES!!!

THE AGE-GUESSER

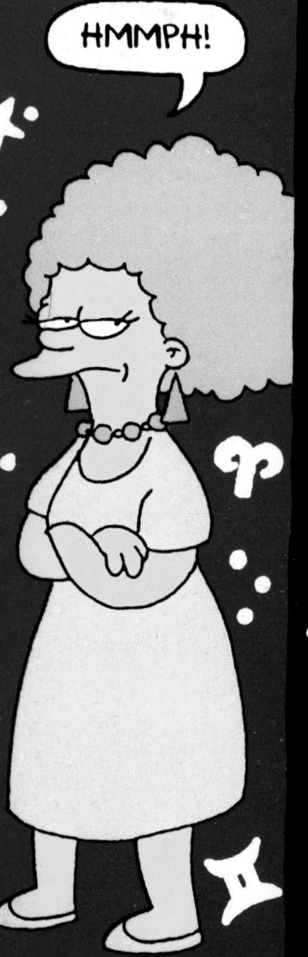
HMMPH!

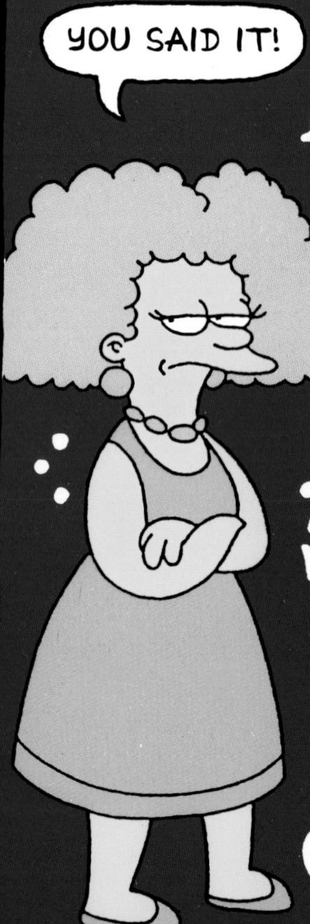
YOU SAID IT!

1	2	4	8	16	32
3	3	5	9	17	33
5	6	6	10	18	34
7	7	7	11	19	35
9	10	12	12	20	36
11	11	13	13	21	37
13	14	14	14	22	38
15	15	15	15	23	39
17	18	20	24	24	40
19	19	21	25	25	41
21	22	22	26	26	42
23	23	23	27	27	43
25	26	28	28	28	44
27	27	29	29	29	45
29	30	30	30	30	46
31	31	31	31	31	47
33	34	36	40	48	48
35	35	37	41	49	49
37	38	38	42	50	50
39	39	39	43	51	51
41	42	44	44	52	52
43	43	45	45	53	53
45	46	46	46	54	54
47	47	47	47	55	55
49	50	52	56	56	56
51	51	53	57	57	57
53	54	54	58	58	58
55	55	55	59	59	59
57	58	60	60	60	60
59	59	61	61	61	61
61	62	62	62	62	62
63	63	63	63	63	63

Ask your friend to tell you which columns his or her age appears in. Add up the numbers at the TOP OF THE COLUMNS indicated and the sum will reveal his or her age. FOR EXAMPLE: Your friend's age is 28. This number, as you see, appears in the third, fourth and fifth columns. The top numbers in those three columns are 4, 8 and 16 – which add up to 28. As the Great Homer-Dini says, "It's easy as pie! It's a piece of cake! Like taking candy from a baby. Enough guessing – let's eat!"

MAGGIE'S MIXED-UP PICTURE SCRAMBLE

MAGGIE'S BEST, BEST PAL IN THE WHOLE WIDE WORLD IS A FABULOUS MONSTER! IT HAS FOUR LEGS, TWO EARS AND ONE GREAT BIG EYE THAT STARES AND GLARES BUT NEVER SEES. CUT THESE PIECES APART AND UNSCRAMBLE THE PICTURE PUZZLE TO DISCOVER MAGGIE'S BEASTLY FRIEND.

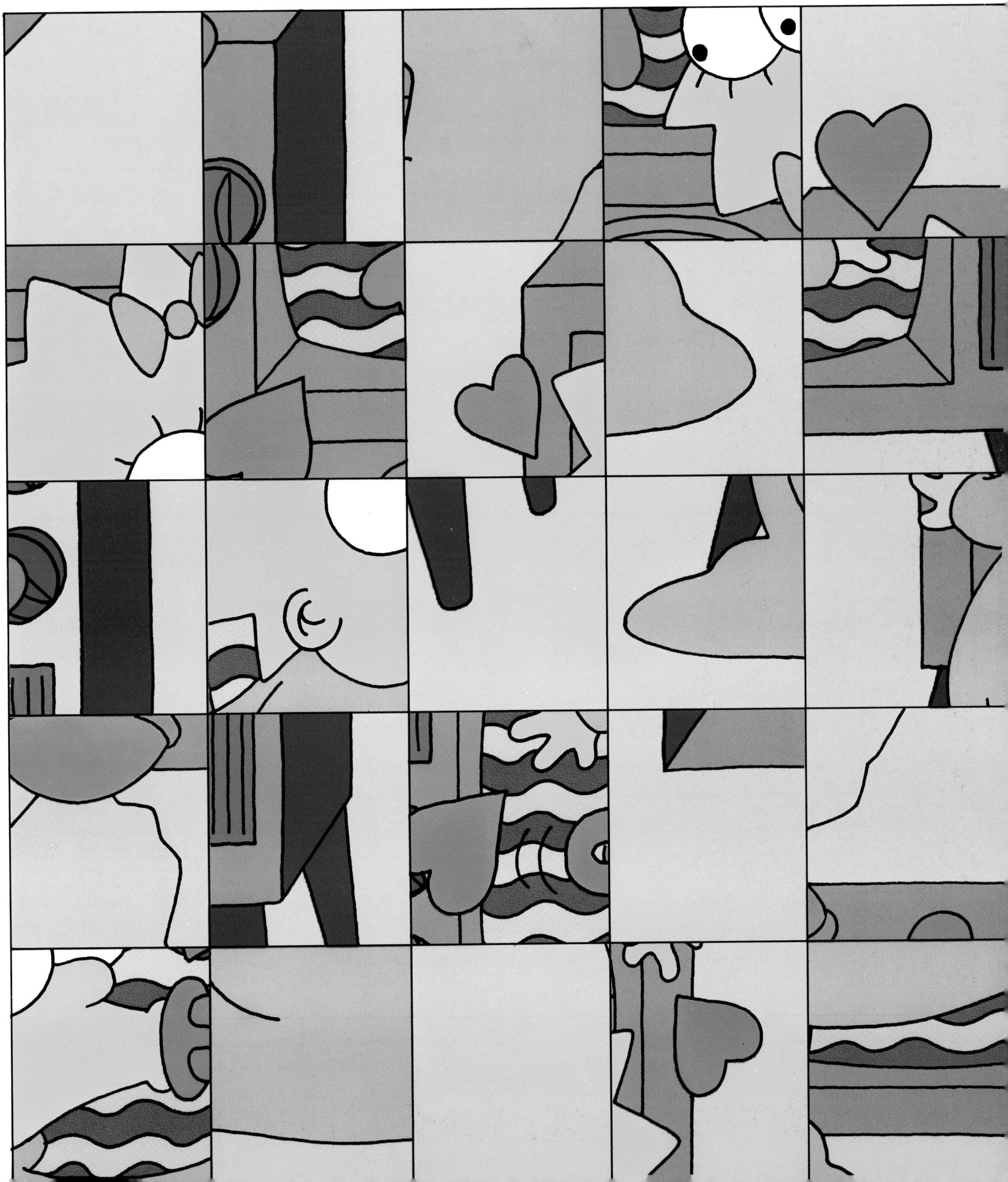

Solution on Page 62.

Pointless Trivia

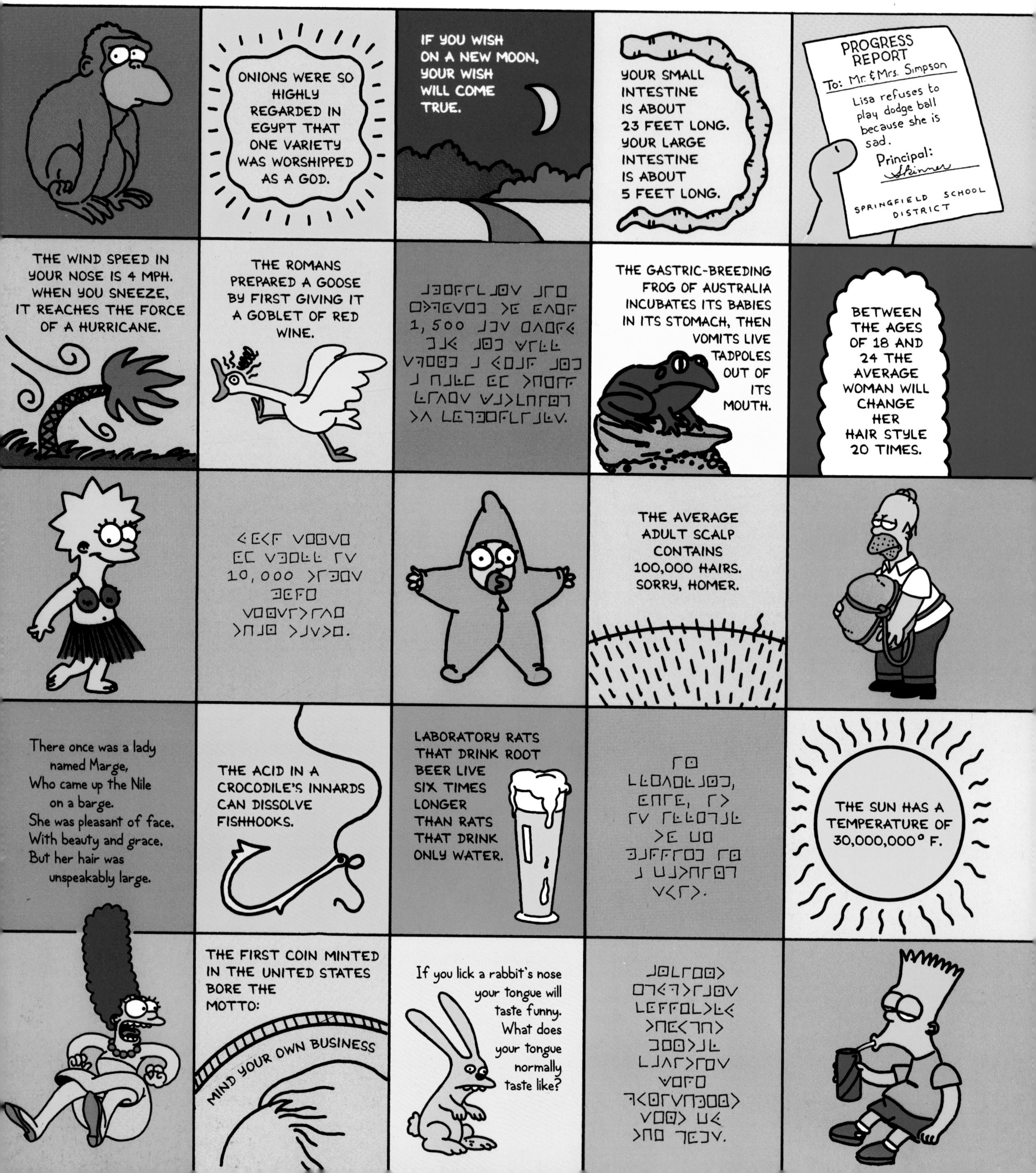

ONIONS WERE SO HIGHLY REGARDED IN EGYPT THAT ONE VARIETY WAS WORSHIPPED AS A GOD.

IF YOU WISH ON A NEW MOON, YOUR WISH WILL COME TRUE.

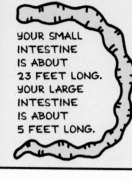

YOUR SMALL INTESTINE IS ABOUT 23 FEET LONG. YOUR LARGE INTESTINE IS ABOUT 5 FEET LONG.

PROGRESS REPORT
To: Mr. & Mrs. Simpson
Lisa refuses to play dodge ball because she is sad.
Principal: Skinner
SPRINGFIELD SCHOOL DISTRICT

THE WIND SPEED IN YOUR NOSE IS 4 MPH. WHEN YOU SNEEZE, IT REACHES THE FORCE OF A HURRICANE.

THE ROMANS PREPARED A GOOSE BY FIRST GIVING IT A GOBLET OF RED WINE.

THE GASTRIC-BREEDING FROG OF AUSTRALIA INCUBATES ITS BABIES IN ITS STOMACH, THEN VOMITS LIVE TADPOLES OUT OF ITS MOUTH.

BETWEEN THE AGES OF 18 AND 24 THE AVERAGE WOMAN WILL CHANGE HER HAIR STYLE 20 TIMES.

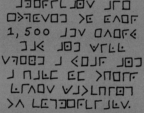

THE AVERAGE ADULT SCALP CONTAINS 100,000 HAIRS. SORRY, HOMER.

There once was a lady named Marge,
Who came up the Nile on a barge.
She was pleasant of face.
With beauty and grace.
But her hair was unspeakably large.

THE ACID IN A CROCODILE'S INNARDS CAN DISSOLVE FISHHOOKS.

LABORATORY RATS THAT DRINK ROOT BEER LIVE SIX TIMES LONGER THAN RATS THAT DRINK ONLY WATER.

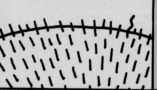

THE SUN HAS A TEMPERATURE OF 30,000,000° F.

THE FIRST COIN MINTED IN THE UNITED STATES BORE THE MOTTO:
MIND YOUR OWN BUSINESS

If you lick a rabbit's nose your tongue will taste funny. What does your tongue normally taste like?

A DAZZLING DYNO-RAMA!

IN SIZZLING SPIN-O-VISION!

ZOETROPE*

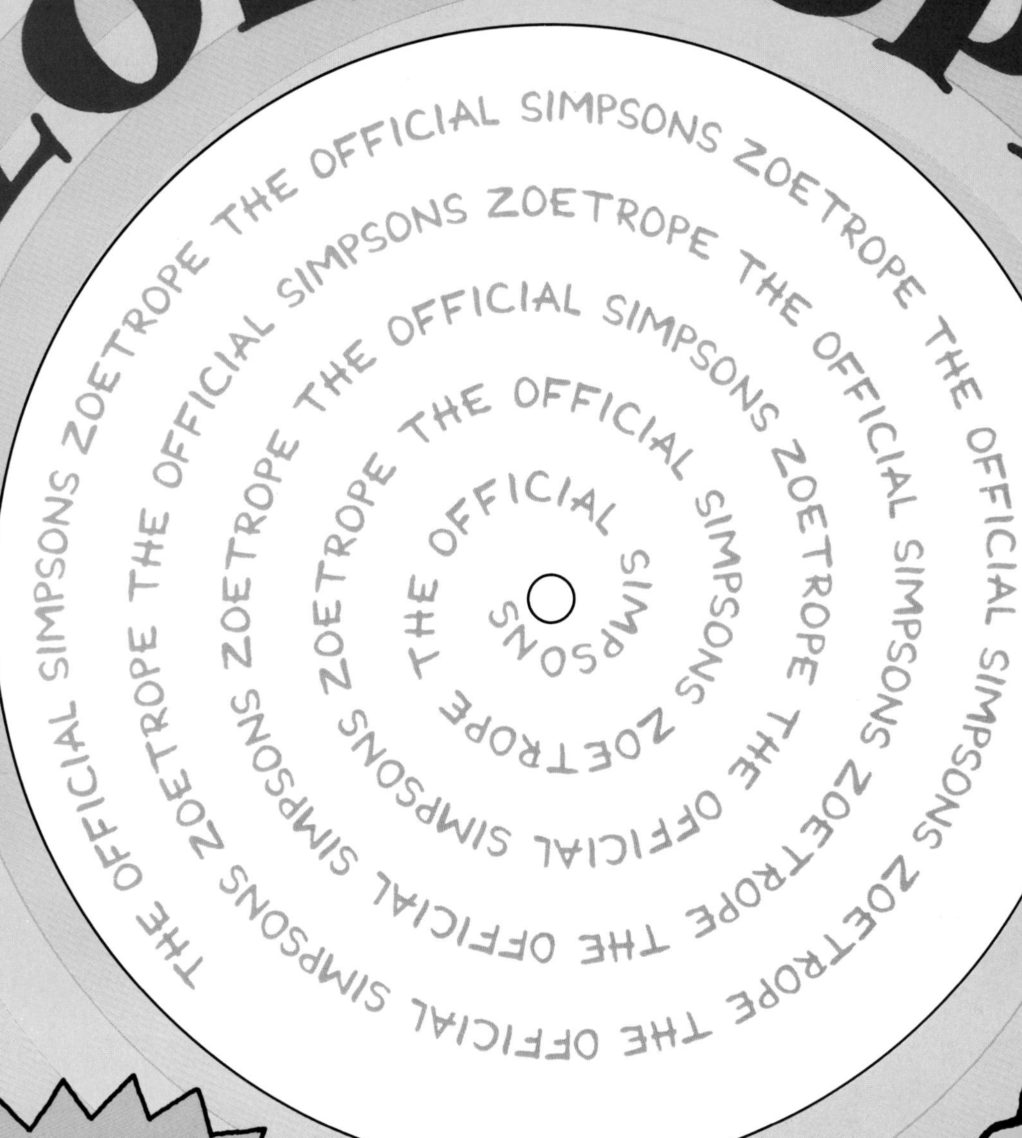
THE OFFICIAL SIMPSONS ZOETROPE

You Will Need...

SCISSORS

TAPE • THUMBTACK

PAPER OR PLASTIC CUP WITH A FLAT BOTTOM

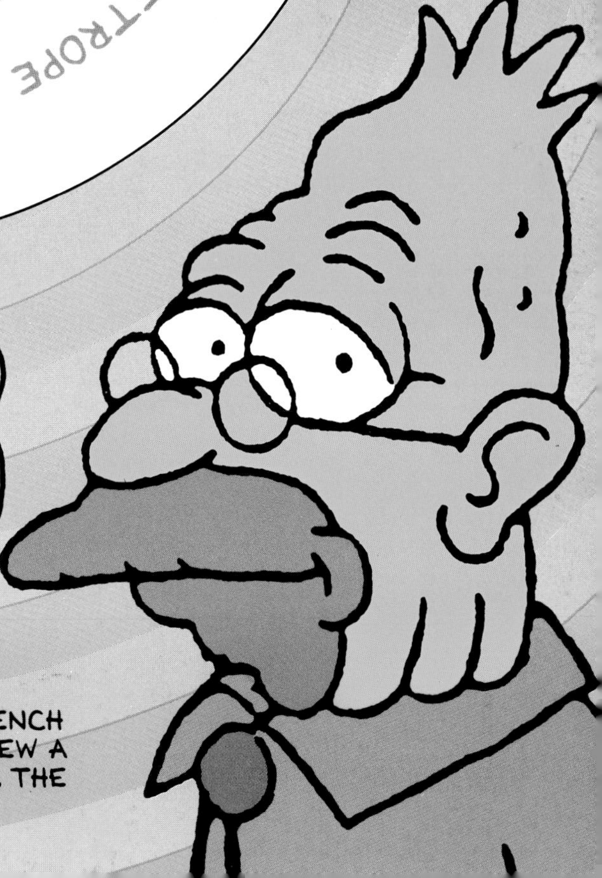
THESE THINGS USED TO MAKE YOUR GRANDMOTHER DIZZY!

* THE ZOETROPE (ZOE-A-TROPE) IS AN OPTICAL TOY THAT CREATES THE ILLUSION OF MOVING PICTURES. THE WORD IS FRENCH FOR "WHEEL OF LIFE." THE ILLUSION IS CREATED WHEN YOU VIEW A SERIES OF DRAWINGS THROUGH SLITS IN A SPINNING CYLINDER. THE DRAWINGS WILL APPEAR TO MOVE LIKE A TINY MOVIE.

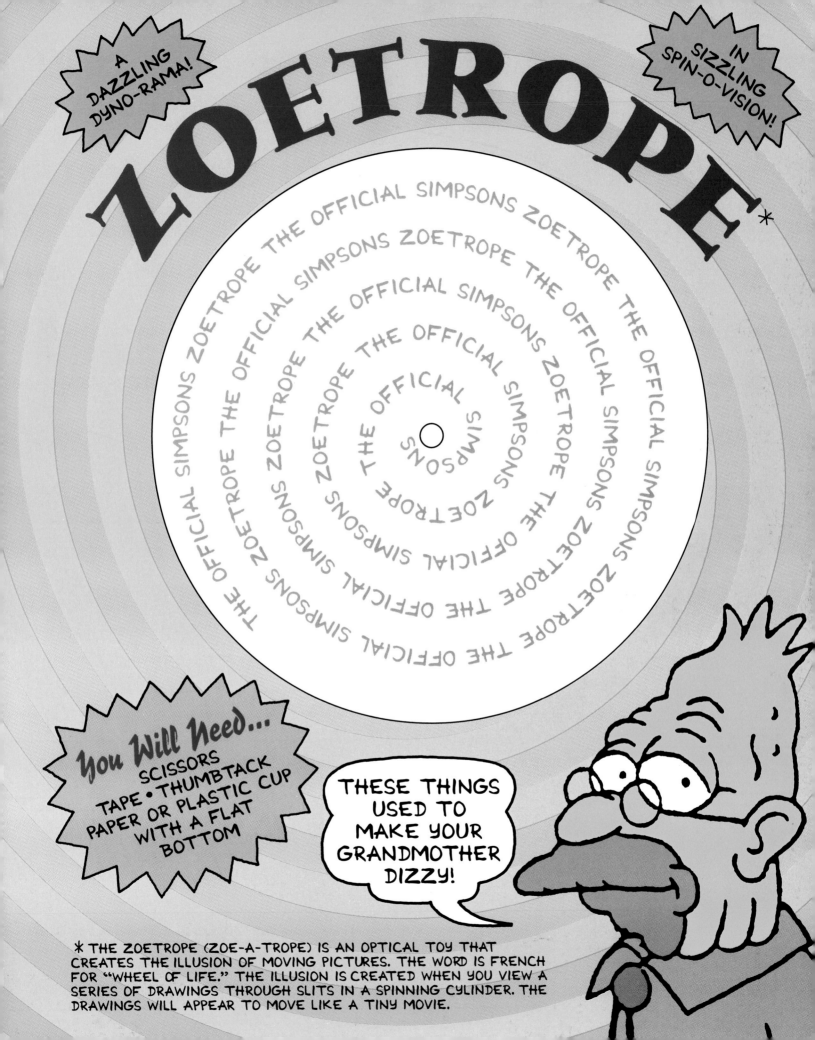

INSTRUCTIONS

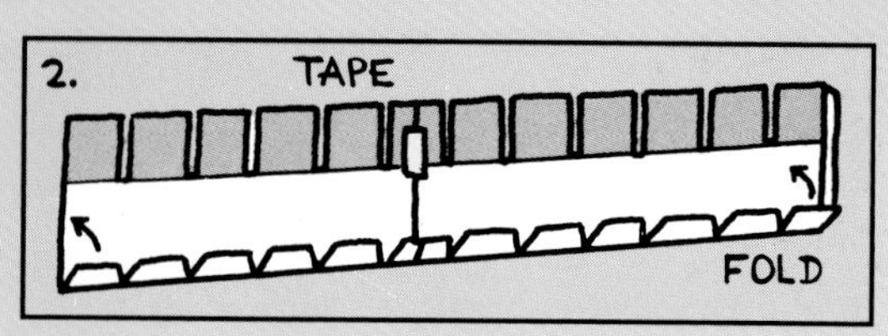
2.
TAPE
FOLD

1. PASTE THE CIRCLE ONTO CARDBOARD AND CUT OUT.

2. CUT OUT THE TWO STRIPS ON THE NEXT PAGE, BEING SURE TO CUT OUT EACH OF THE LITTLE SLITS, TOO. TAPE THE STRIPS TOGETHER AND FOLD UP THE BOTTOM TABS AS SHOWN.

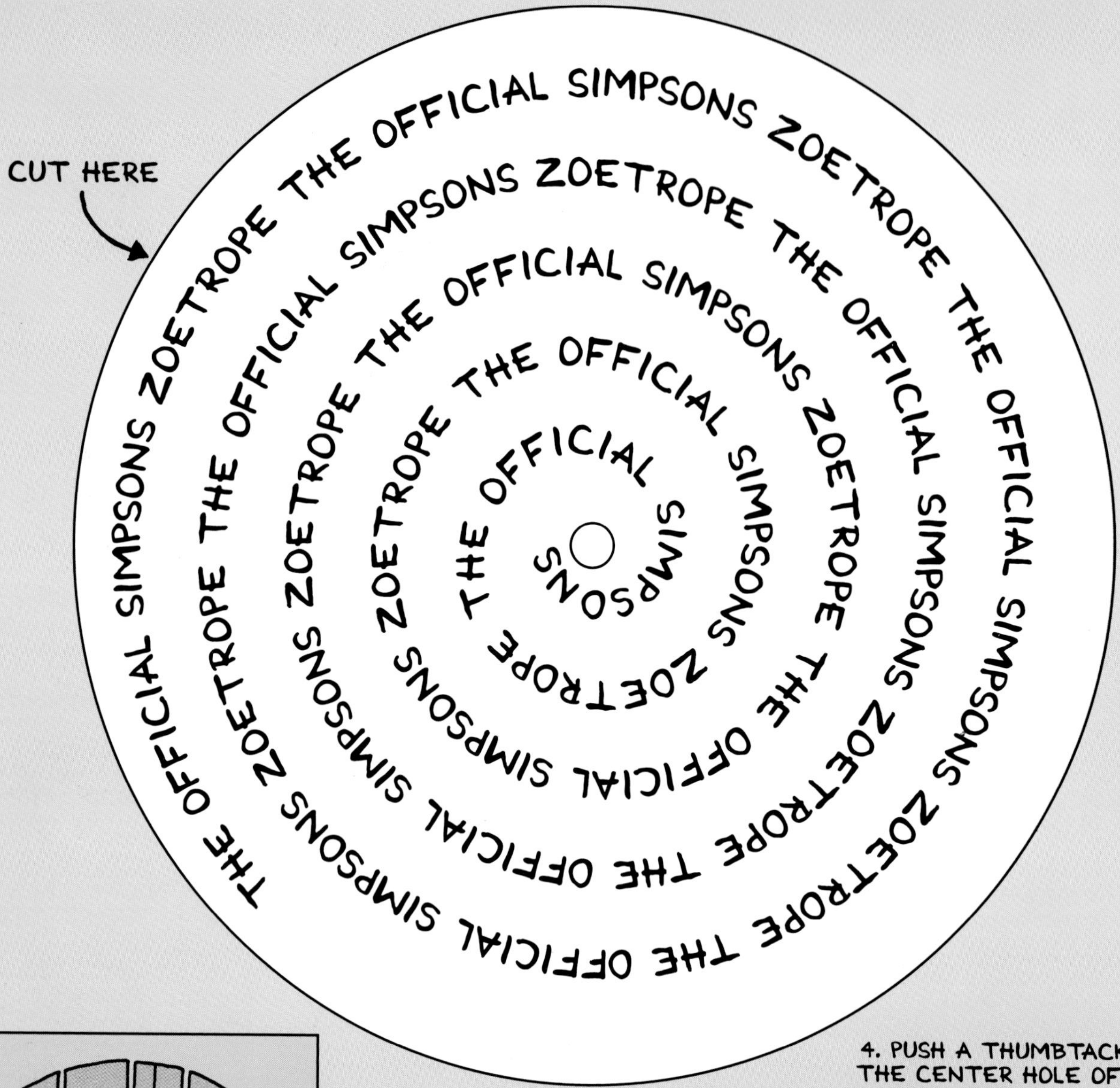
CUT HERE
THE OFFICIAL SIMPSONS ZOETROPE

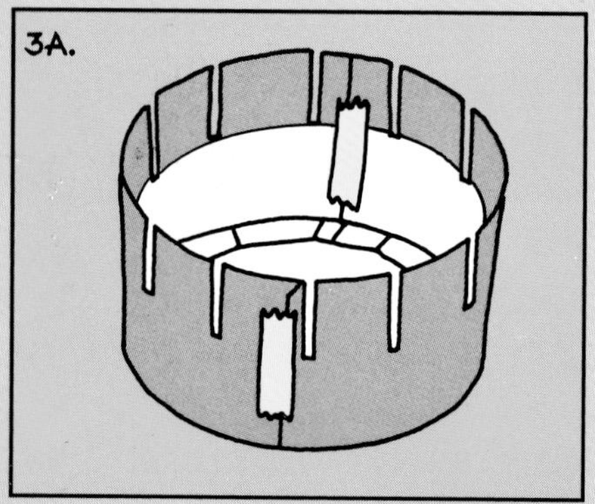
3A.

3. TAPE THE ENDS OF THE STRIP TOGETHER WITH THE BLACK SIDE OUT. DROP THE CIRCLE DOWN INTO IT AND TAPE THE WHOLE THING TOGETHER ON THE BOTTOM.

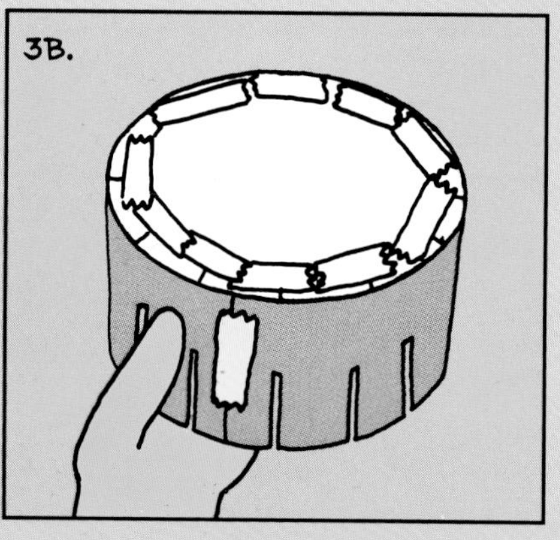
3B.

4. PUSH A THUMBTACK THROUGH THE CENTER HOLE OF THE BASE AND ATTACH IT TO A PLASTIC SPRAY CAN TOP OR A PLASTIC CUP.

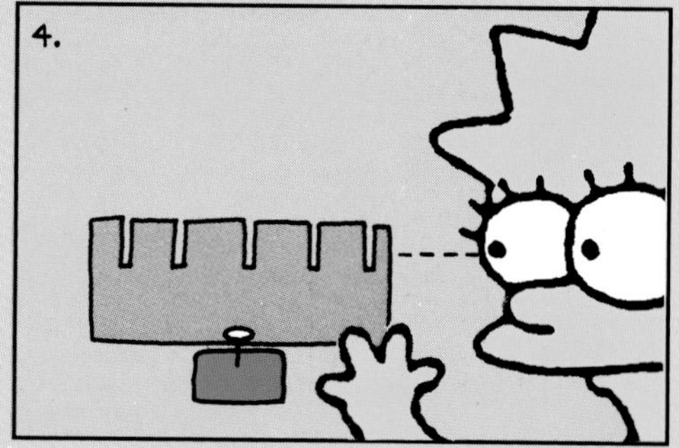
4.

HOLD IT AT EYE LEVEL IN BRIGHT LIGHT, LOOK THROUGH THE SLITS AND SPIN!

5. FOR MORE MOVING PICTURES, CUT OUT THE OTHER STRIPS ON THE FOLLOWING PAGES AND TAPE THEM TOGETHER AS INDICATED. PLACE ONE OF THEM INSIDE THE "WHEEL OF LIFE" AND SPIN AS YOU DID BEFORE. TO SEE THE OTHER SIDES OF THE STRIPS, CUT THE TAPE, TURN THE STRIP AROUND AND TAPE IT AGAIN.

CUT ALONG LINES. ATTACH A TO A AND B TO B.

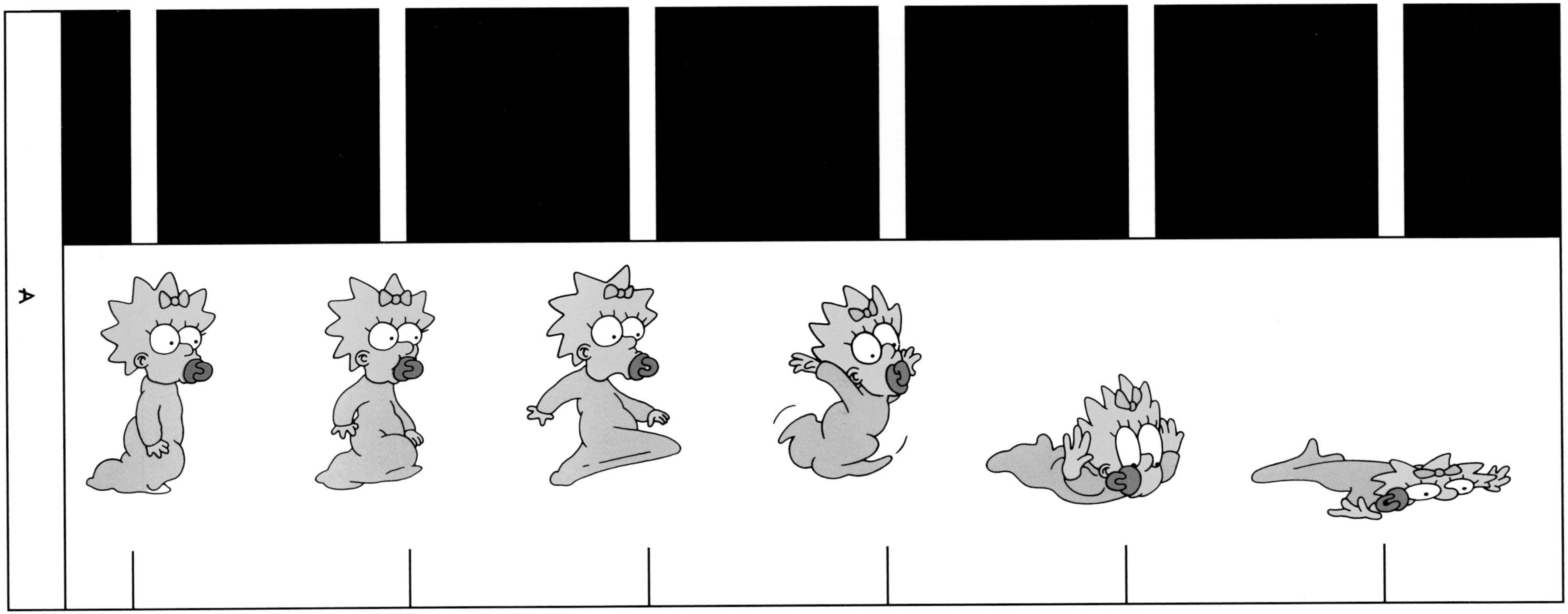

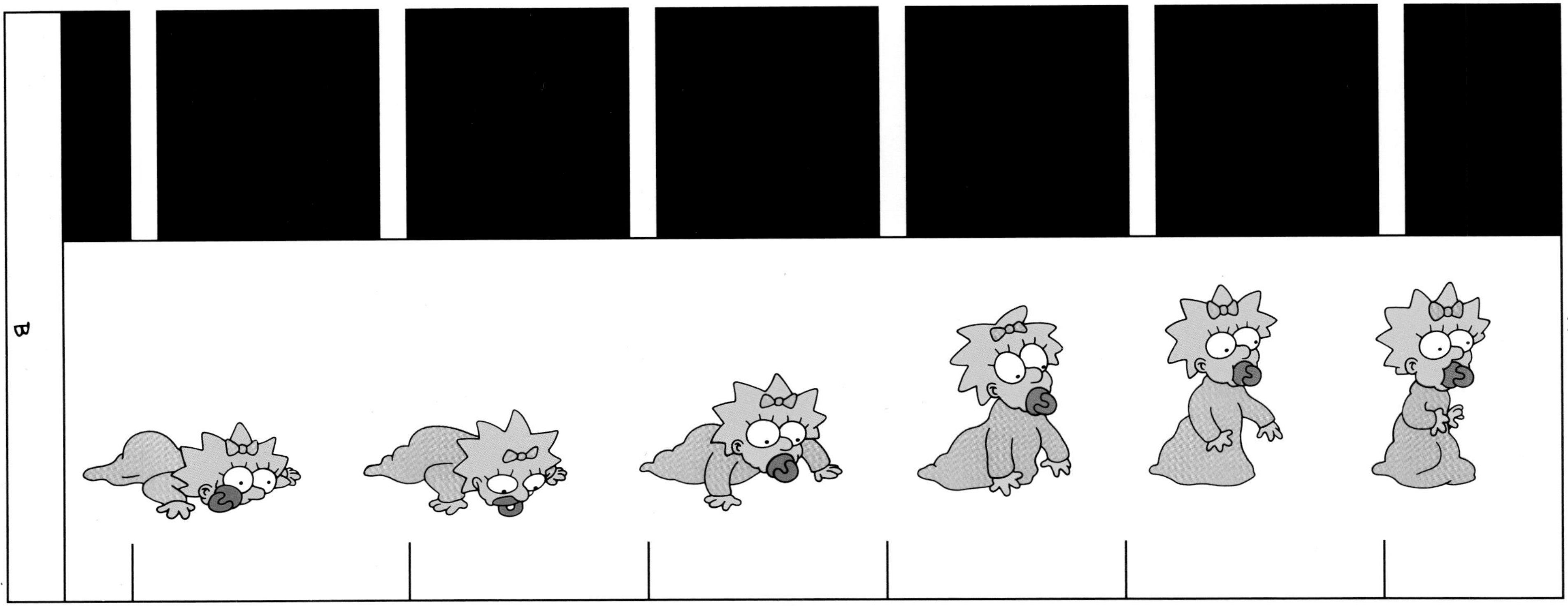

CUT ALONG LINES. ATTACH A TO A AND B TO B.

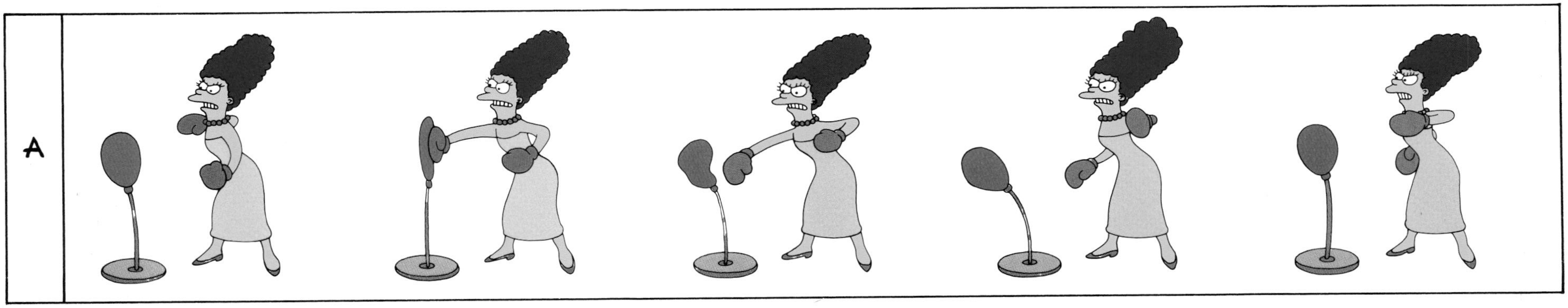
A
B

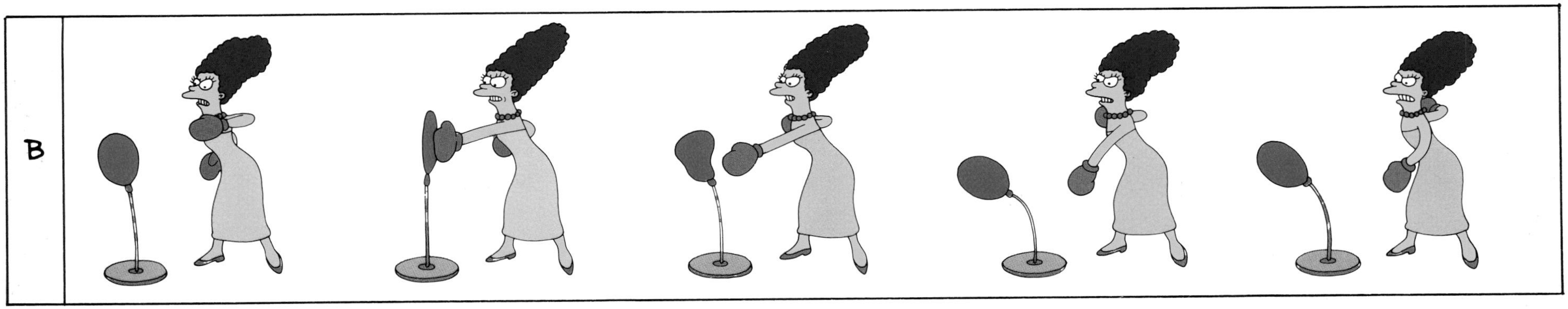
B
A

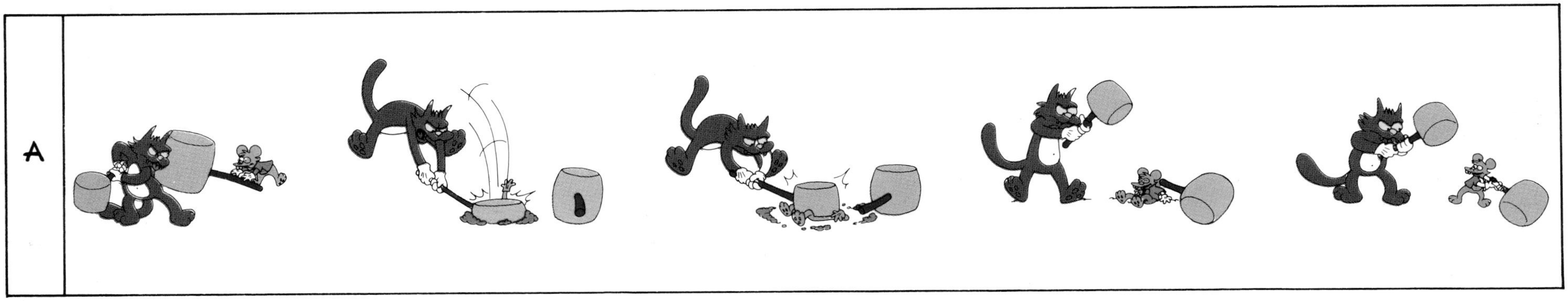
A
B

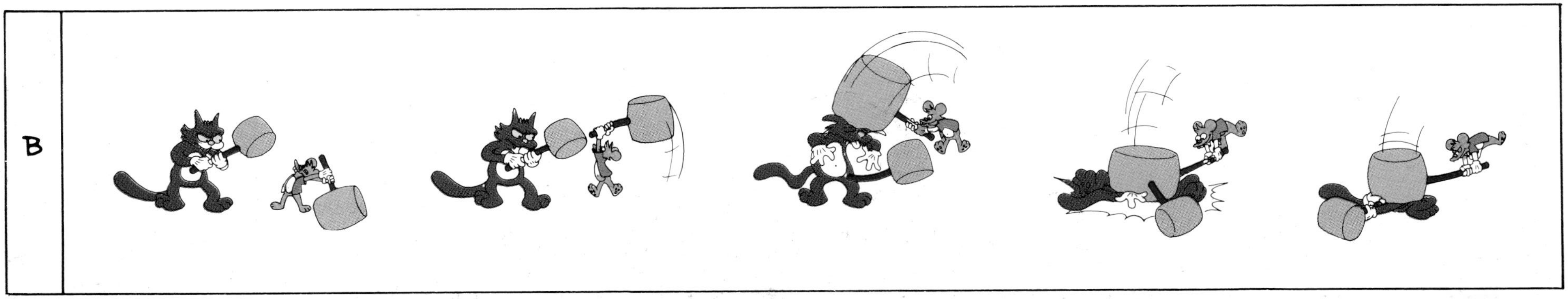
B
A

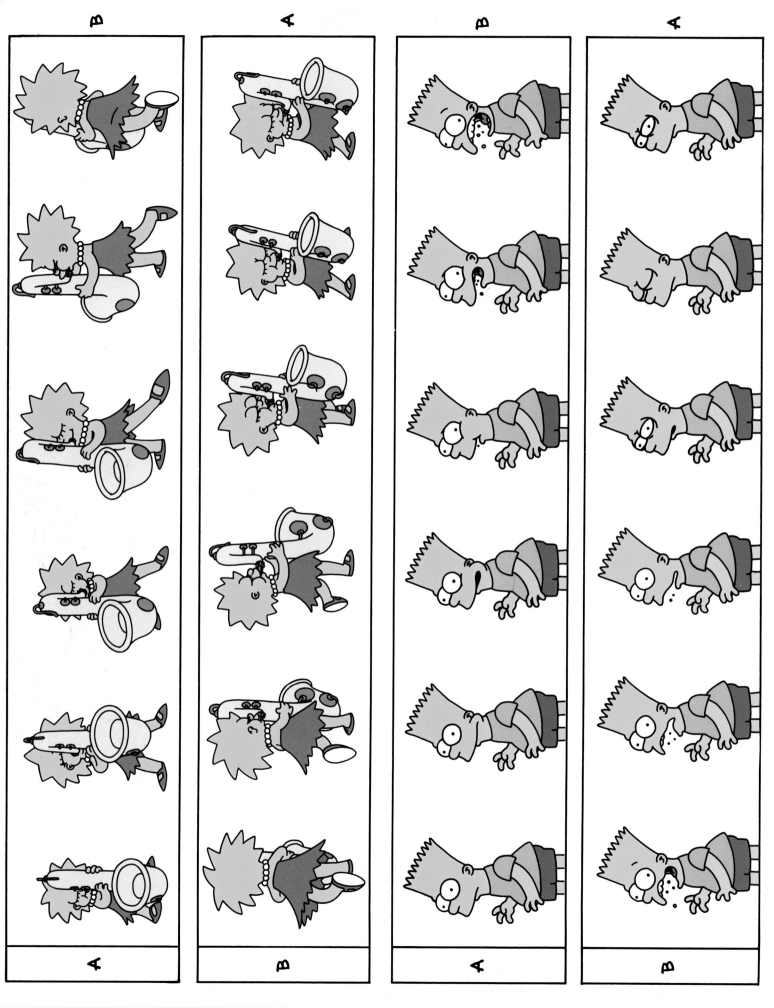

CUT ALONG LINES. ATTACH A TO A AND B TO B.

PICNIC PANIC!

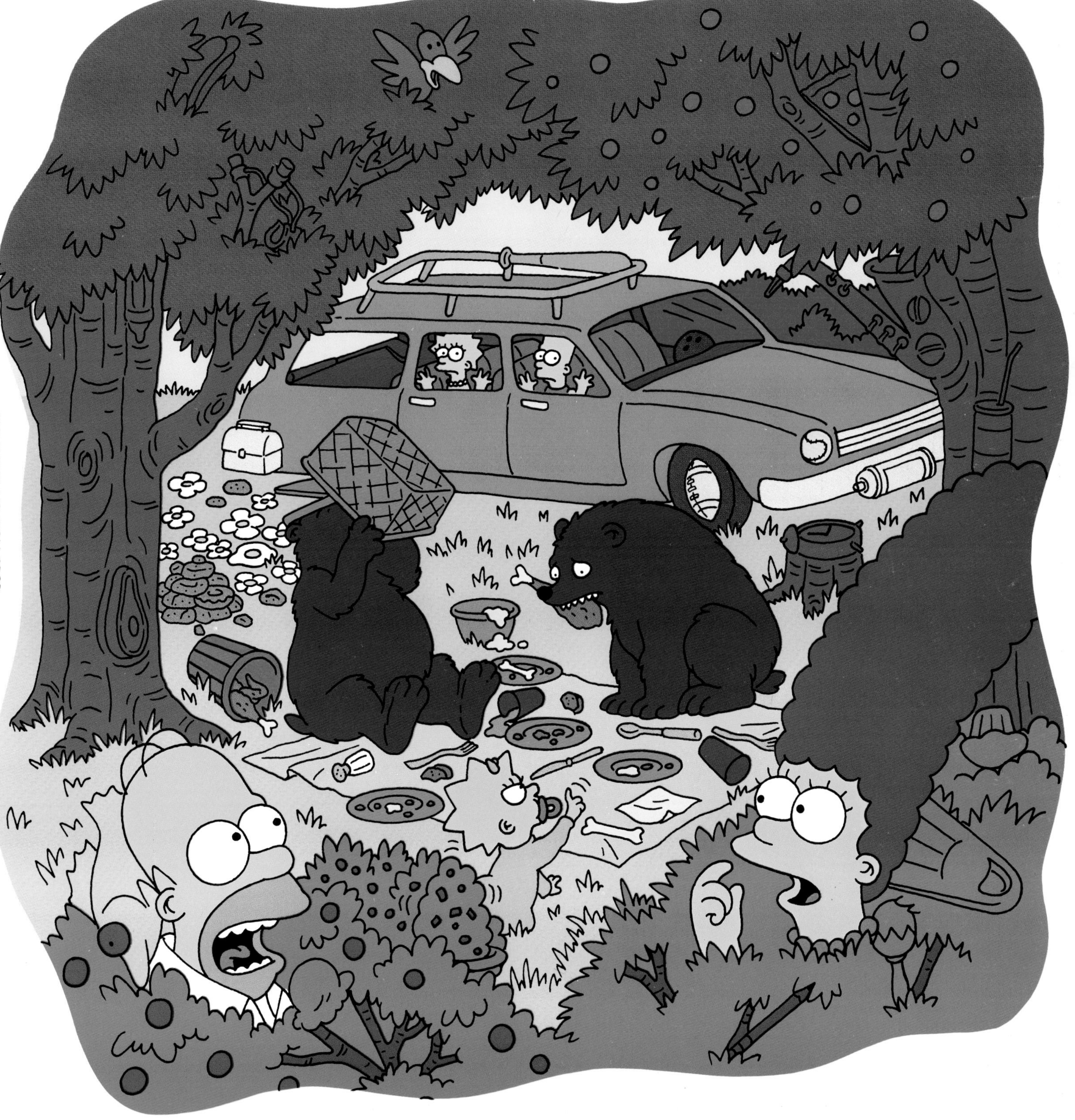

SOLUTION ON PAGE 62.

Those darn bears have scattered 24 items from the Simpsons' picnic all over the woods! Can you help find them all?

ESCAPE from 4TH GRADE

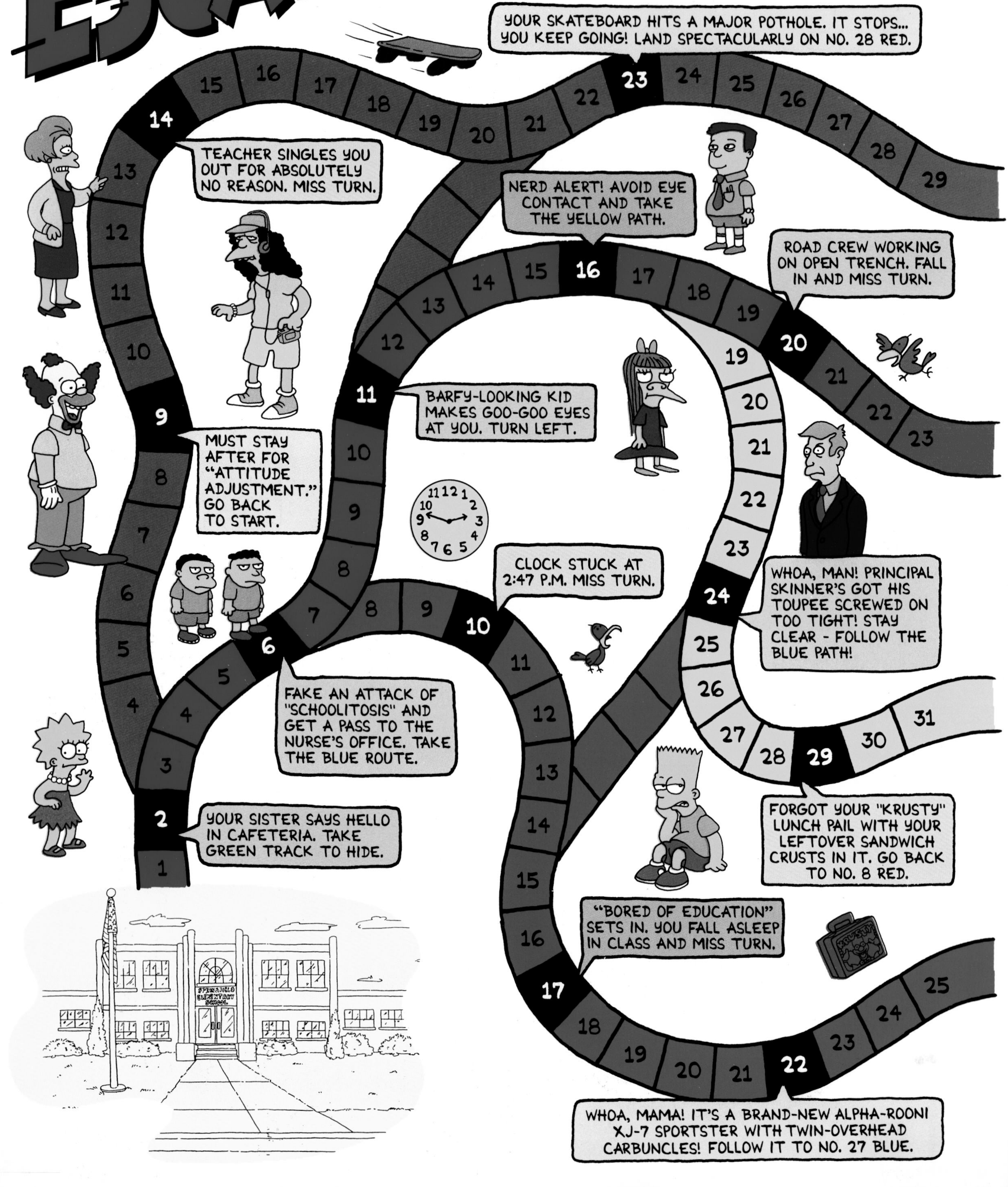
YOUR SISTER SAYS HELLO IN CAFETERIA. TAKE GREEN TRACK TO HIDE.
FAKE AN ATTACK OF "SCHOOLITOSIS" AND GET A PASS TO THE NURSE'S OFFICE. TAKE THE BLUE ROUTE.
MUST STAY AFTER FOR "ATTITUDE ADJUSTMENT." GO BACK TO START.
TEACHER SINGLES YOU OUT FOR ABSOLUTELY NO REASON. MISS TURN.
BARFY-LOOKING KID MAKES GOO-GOO EYES AT YOU. TURN LEFT.
CLOCK STUCK AT 2:47 P.M. MISS TURN.
NERD ALERT! AVOID EYE CONTACT AND TAKE THE YELLOW PATH.
YOUR SKATEBOARD HITS A MAJOR POTHOLE. IT STOPS... YOU KEEP GOING! LAND SPECTACULARLY ON NO. 28 RED.
ROAD CREW WORKING ON OPEN TRENCH. FALL IN AND MISS TURN.
WHOA, MAN! PRINCIPAL SKINNER'S GOT HIS TOUPEE SCREWED ON TOO TIGHT! STAY CLEAR - FOLLOW THE BLUE PATH!
FORGOT YOUR "KRUSTY" LUNCH PAIL WITH YOUR LEFTOVER SANDWICH CRUSTS IN IT. GO BACK TO NO. 8 RED.
"BORED OF EDUCATION" SETS IN. YOU FALL ASLEEP IN CLASS AND MISS TURN.
WHOA, MAMA! IT'S A BRAND-NEW ALPHA-ROONI XJ-7 SPORTSTER WITH TWIN-OVERHEAD CARBUNCLES! FOLLOW IT TO NO. 27 BLUE.

HELP BART GET HOME AS FAST AS POSSIBLE! A GAME FOR 2 OR MORE PLAYERS. EACH PLAYER THROWS A DIE IN TURN AND MOVES FORWARD THE NUMBER ROLLED. THE EXACT NUMBER MUST BE THROWN TO REACH "HOME." EACH PLAYER USES A DIFFERENT COLOR BUTTON OR MARKER.

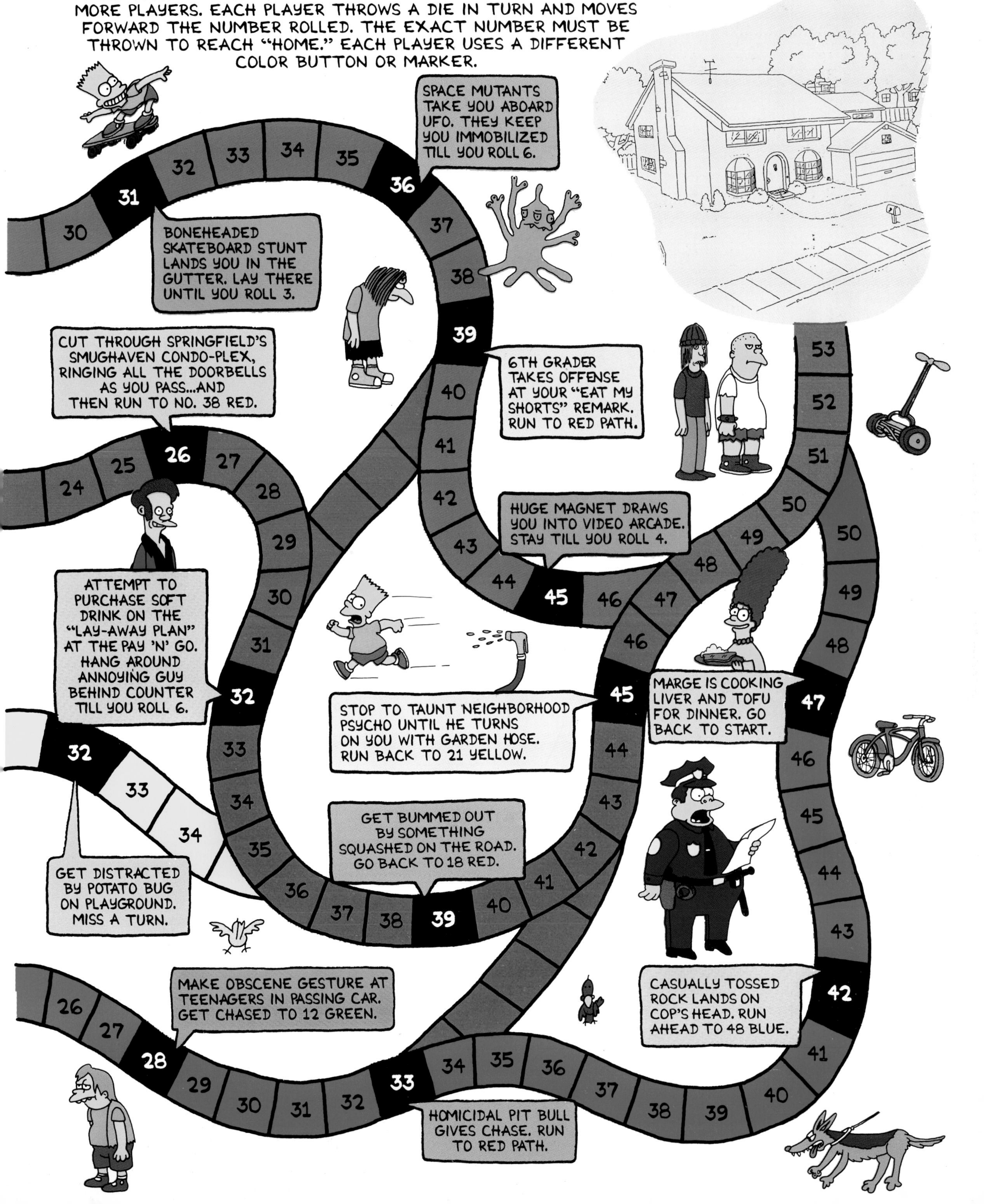
BONEHEADED SKATEBOARD STUNT LANDS YOU IN THE GUTTER. LAY THERE UNTIL YOU ROLL 3.
SPACE MUTANTS TAKE YOU ABOARD UFO. THEY KEEP YOU IMMOBILIZED TILL YOU ROLL 6.
6TH GRADER TAKES OFFENSE AT YOUR "EAT MY SHORTS" REMARK. RUN TO RED PATH.
HUGE MAGNET DRAWS YOU INTO VIDEO ARCADE. STAY TILL YOU ROLL 4.
CUT THROUGH SPRINGFIELD'S SMUGHAVEN CONDO-PLEX, RINGING ALL THE DOORBELLS AS YOU PASS...AND THEN RUN TO NO. 38 RED.
ATTEMPT TO PURCHASE SOFT DRINK ON THE "LAY-AWAY PLAN" AT THE PAY 'N' GO. HANG AROUND ANNOYING GUY BEHIND COUNTER TILL YOU ROLL 6.
GET BUMMED OUT BY SOMETHING SQUASHED ON THE ROAD. GO BACK TO 18 RED.
STOP TO TAUNT NEIGHBORHOOD PSYCHO UNTIL HE TURNS ON YOU WITH GARDEN HOSE. RUN BACK TO 21 YELLOW.
GET DISTRACTED BY POTATO BUG ON PLAYGROUND. MISS A TURN.
MAKE OBSCENE GESTURE AT TEENAGERS IN PASSING CAR. GET CHASED TO 12 GREEN.
HOMICIDAL PIT BULL GIVES CHASE. RUN TO RED PATH.
CASUALLY TOSSED ROCK LANDS ON COP'S HEAD. RUN AHEAD TO 48 BLUE.
MARGE IS COOKING LIVER AND TOFU FOR DINNER. GO BACK TO START.

The Simpsons Take a Road Trip

Write each item from the list on a 3" x 5" index card and deal the cards out to all the players. The narrator reads the story, pausing at the blanks. In turn, each player reads a card to fill in the missing words.

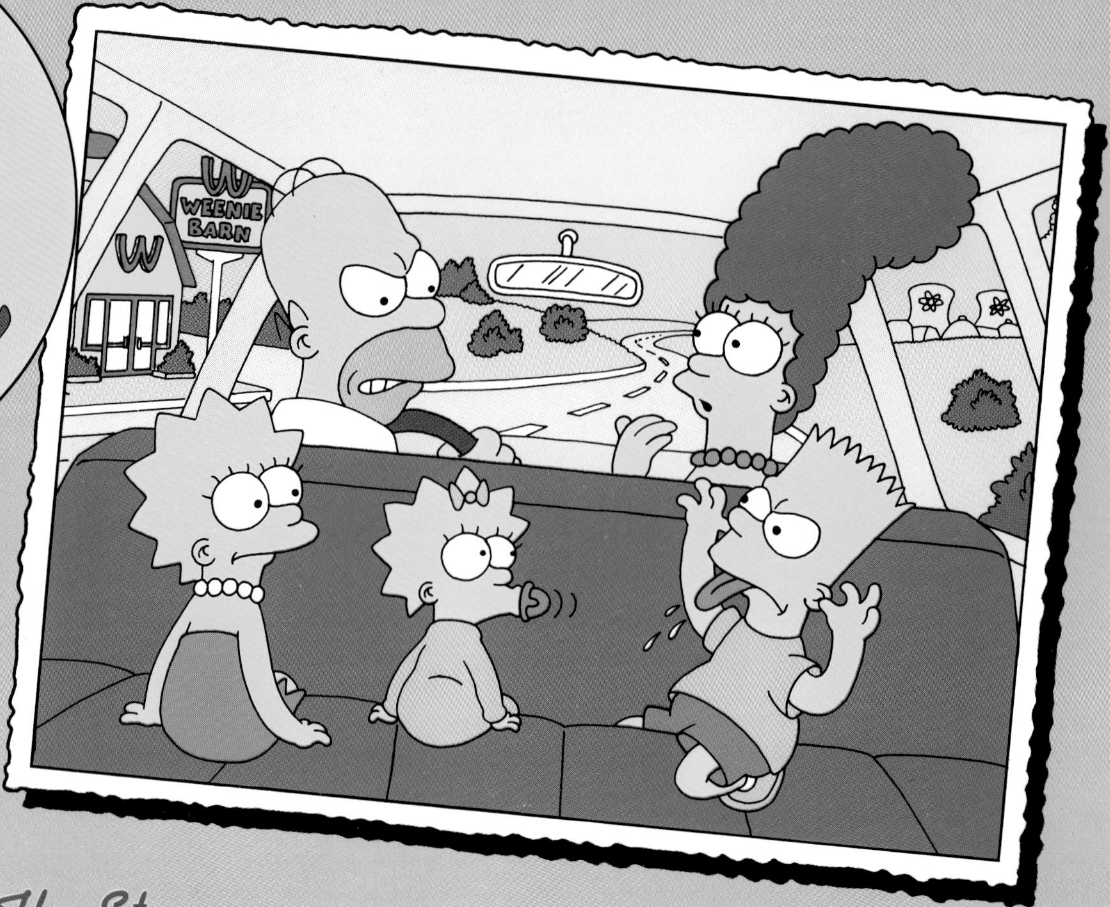
WEENIE BARN

The List

a cheap cigar
a space mutant
six fur balls
a snide remark
a knuckle sandwich
a smug poodle
a tofu salad
a ridiculous hair style
a frozen pizza
a screaming lunatic
a jar of dirt
a cow pie
two stupid cats
a garden slug
a wharf rat
a young Republican
a pain in the butt
a nuclear bomb
an excitable hamster
a rusted accordion
a big, phony smile
a greasy doorknob
forty-two jelly donuts
a dull thud
a smelly, old sock

The Story

Like it or not, it's time for the Simpsons' annual vacation road trip. Or, as Bart calls it, "Bummer in the Summer." Homer has loaded up the car with ______, ______ and ______. And Marge has prepared ______, ______ and ______to eat along the way.

Soon they're all packed up and heading down the highway. "Oh, look!" says Lisa, pointing out the window. "There's a car with ______ strapped to its roof!" "They must be from California," reasons Marge.

"Dad, I'm so hungry I could eat______!" says Bart. "Let's stop at that Weenie Barn up ahead!" Homer pulls in and everyone piles out of the car. "I'll get us a booth near ______," says Bart as he charges into the restaurant.

"Welcome to Weenie Barn," says the waitress. "Today's special is ______served on ______. So, what kin I get youse guys?" "I'll have ______, ______ and ______!" shouts Bart. "And I'll have ______, ______ and______," says Lisa. "Cool it, you two," says Homer. "Your eyes are bigger than your stomachs. We'll just have ______ each and a side of juicy fries," says Marge. "Oh, and ______ for Maggie."

The scrumptious meal is quickly eaten. "C'mon," says Homer. "I wanna put in another 200 miles before dark." Unfortunately, when they all get back in the car, it won't start. "Sounds like you got ______in the carburetor, Dad," observes Bart. "Drat!" curses Homer. "I KNEW I shoulda put ______in the radiator before we left!" "Yes, dear," says Marge calmly. "That's why I put a spare one in the trunk."

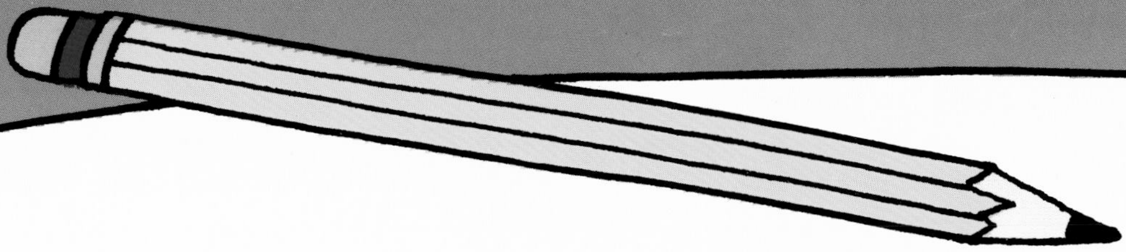

PENCIL PAGE

HANGMAN

One player is the executioner. The other is the convict. The executioner thinks of a 6- or 7-letter word and marks down a dash for each letter on some paper. The convict tries to guess, one by one, the letters that make up the word. For each wrong guess, the executioner draws in a part of the gallows or the hanging man. First the gallows, then the rope, then the head, the face, the body, the left arm, the right arm, the left leg and the right leg. If the convict guesses a letter in the word, the executioner writes it in position on the dash. If the convict guesses the whole word before he is hanged, he wins. If not, the executioner wins. If you choose an especially long or tough word, you can add more body parts (ears, eyes, etc.) to give the convict a reprieve on his sentence.

							7	8	9	10
1	2		3	4	5	6				
							17	18	19	
11	12	13		14	15	16				
						26		27	28	29
20	21	22	23		24	25				

DOUBLE ACROSTIC: ANSWER EACH OF THE QUESTIONS BELOW. THEN ENTER THE LETTERS INTO THE BOXES ABOVE ACCORDING TO THE NUMBERS INDICATED.

A. Word before dog or foot or rod. ___15 ___12 ___6

B. Weak; spineless. ___14 ___1 ___9 ___10 ___27

C. Head of the House of Simpson. ___20 ___16 ___2 ___26 ___5

D. What Bart is to the above. ___7 ___28 ___13

E. John or Paul or George or Ringo. ___3 ___19 ___24 ___17 ___23 ___21

F. Ben's last name. ___18 ___29 ___25

G. Simpson sibling. ___22 ___8 ___11 ___4

Solutions on page 62.

WHOEVER REACHES THE TV FIRST GETS TO PICK THE CHANNEL. WILL IT BE AMERICA'S MOST ARMED AND DANGEROUS OR THE HAPPY LITTLE ELVES?

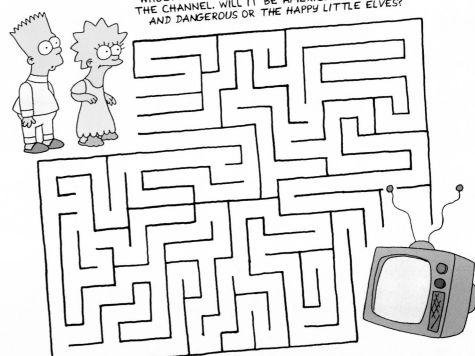

Lisa's HOUSE O' MYSTERIES

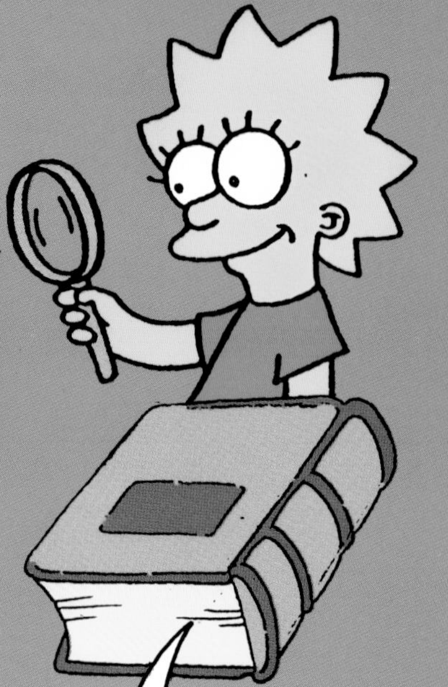

TREASURE HUNT

First, pick out a "treasure" and hide it somewhere in the house. Then, write the clues on pieces of paper and hide them around the house. Each clue tells where to find the next clue, right up to the treasure. The first clue is read aloud to all players. This hunt starts with: "I light up your life!"

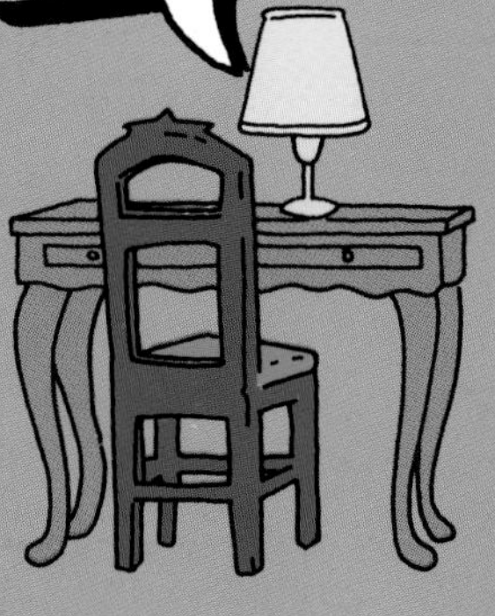

"I have SPOKE, but said nothing. Come AROUND and you'll find clue #3."

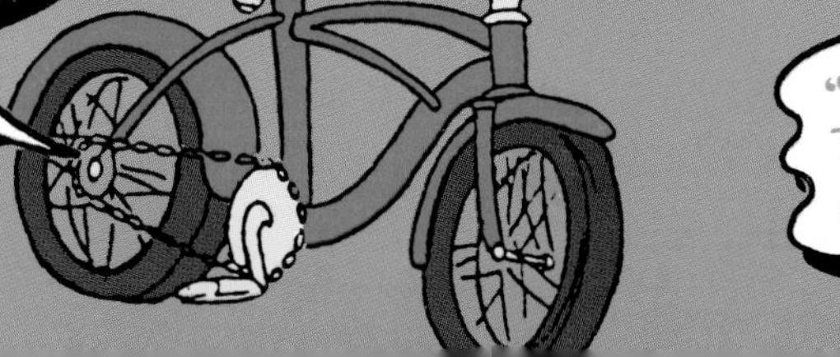

"I never move, yet you're always WATCHING ME. Look to me for clue #4."

MURDER IN THE DARK

THIS IS A GOOD GAME FOR 5 OR MORE PLAYERS. FIRST, CUT SLIPS OF PAPER FOR EACH PLAYER. MARK AN "X" ON ONE PIECE AND A "D" ON ANOTHER. ALL THE REST ARE LEFT BLANK. FOLD THEM IN HALF AND HAVE EACH PLAYER TAKE ONE. THE PLAYER WITH THE "X" IS THE MURDERER. HE KEEPS IT A SECRET. "D" IS THE DETECTIVE. HE TELLS EVERYONE WHO HE IS.

NEXT, THE LIGHTS ARE TURNED OFF AND EVERYONE EXCEPT THE DETECTIVE HIDES. THE MURDERER SNEAKS UP ON A HIDDEN PLAYER AND WHISPERS "YOU'RE DEAD" AND RUNS OFF. THE VICTIM SCREAMS, THE LIGHTS ARE TURNED ON AND EVERYONE GATHERS AROUND HIM. THE DETECTIVE THEN ASKS QUESTIONS TO FIND OUT WHO DONE IT. ONLY THE MURDERER CAN LIE. THE DETECTIVE HAS 3 GUESSES TO IDENTIFY THE MURDERER.

DETECTIVE

TWO PLAYERS ARE SELECTED TO BE DETECTIVES. THEY ARE THEN SENT OUT OF THE ROOM. THE OTHERS CHOOSE AN OBJECT WHICH THE DETECTIVES WILL TRY TO DISCOVER. THIS CAN BE A BOOK, A CHAIR, PART OF SOMEONE'S CLOTHING OR ANYTHING IN THE ROOM. THE DETECTIVES ARE CALLED BACK IN AND TRY TO SOLVE THE MYSTERY BY ASKING QUESTIONS. THEY MAY ASK EACH PLAYER ONLY 3 QUESTIONS. HAVE THEM TRY TO FIND THE LOCATION FIRST, AND THEN ATTEMPT TO NAME THE OBJECT.

ANSWER: The treasure is under "TREASURE" in the dictionary!

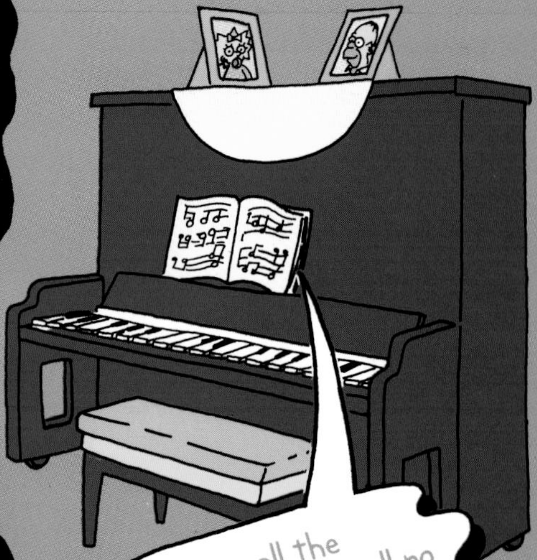

"I know all the WORDS, but I tell no story. Look me up and find the 'treasure'!"

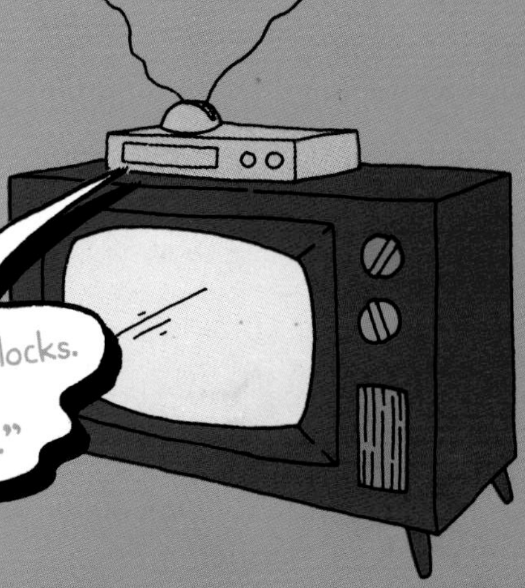

"I have KEYS, but no locks. Take NOTE and you'll discover your next clue."

WHO SWIPED THE CUPCAKES?

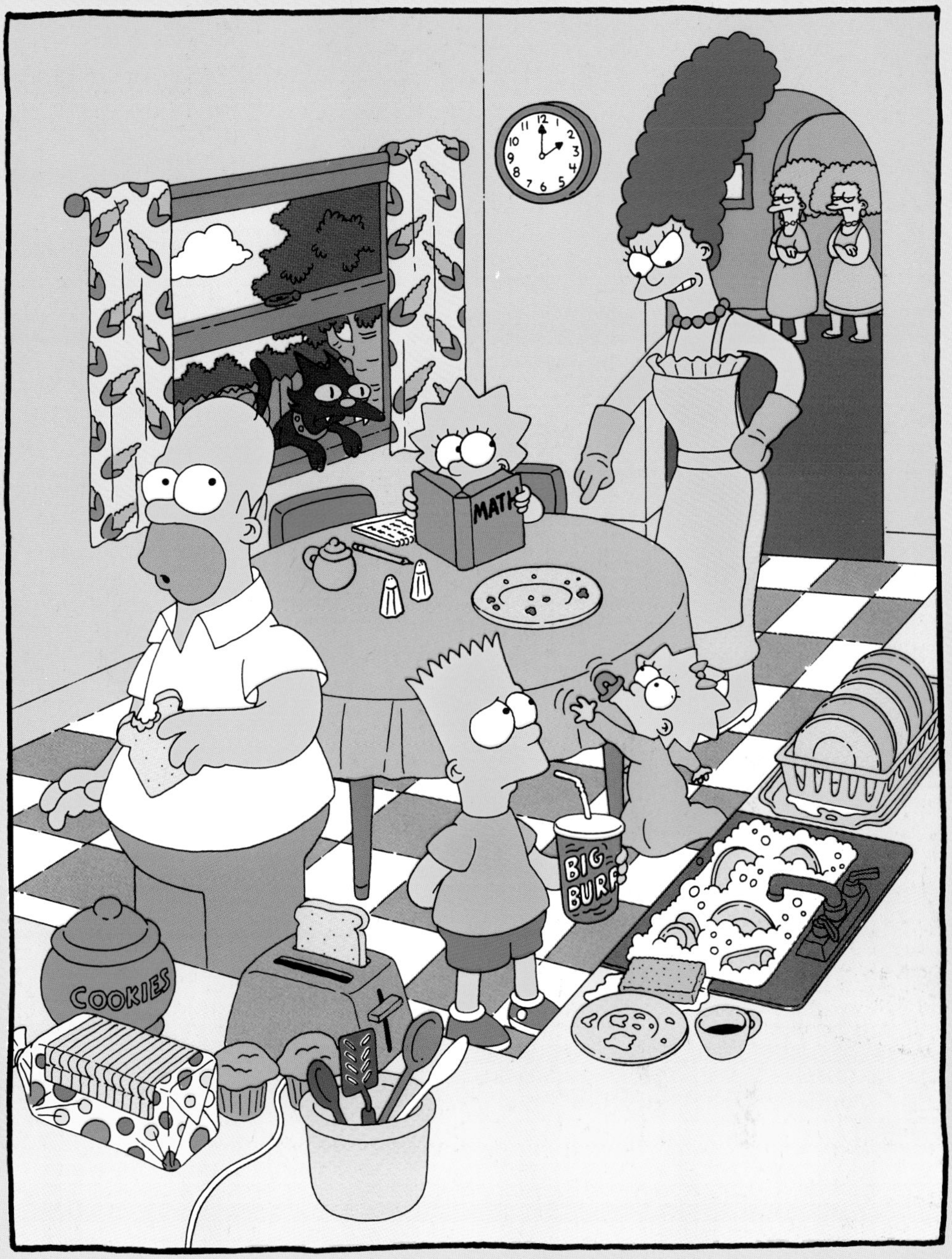
MATH
BIG BURP
COOKIES

Marge had invited her sisters, Patty and Selma, over for a visit...just a little chit-chat and "girl talk." They said they'd be over around 2 o'clock.

The Simpsons had eaten a nutritious lunch a short while ago and there were two yummy cupcakes left over. "Mmmmm," said Marge. "I'll serve these to Patty and Selma when they arrive." She placed the cupcakes on a plate on the kitchen table and then went about cleaning up the kitchen. Maggie was crawling about on the floor, Lisa was quietly doing her homework, Bart was slurping on a "Big Burp" soda and Homer was milling about nearby.

Promptly at 2 o'clock the doorbell rang. "I'll get it," said Marge. "It must be my sisters!"

"Hooo-boy," moaned Homer. "Those two brighten a room just by leaving it!"

Marge put the dish she was washing in the dish rack and went to the front door. On her way past the kitchen table she checked once more on the two yummy cupcakes.

When Marge opened the door to greet Patty and Selma she realized she still had on her rubber dishwashing gloves. "Oh dear!" cried Marge. "Make yourselves at home, girls! I'll be right back!" When Marge dashed back into the kitchen she saw right away that the two cupcakes had disappeared. "Oh my word! In the mere 30 seconds I was out of this room someone swiped those two yummy cupcakes!"

The drawing shows the kitchen immediately upon Marge's return. Can you tell who swiped the cupcakes and how the thief tried to cover his or her tracks?

1. Was it easy for Maggie to grab the cupcakes?
2. Was it easy to Lisa to grab the cupcakes?
3. Was it easy for Bart to grab the cupcakes?
4. Was it easy for Homer to grab the cupcakes?
5. Do you see anyone else who might have taken them?
6. Do you see any place the cupcakes might be hidden?
7. Do you see any clue as to who might have hidden them there?
8. If so, who do you think swiped the cupcakes and how can you tell?

Solution on Page 62.

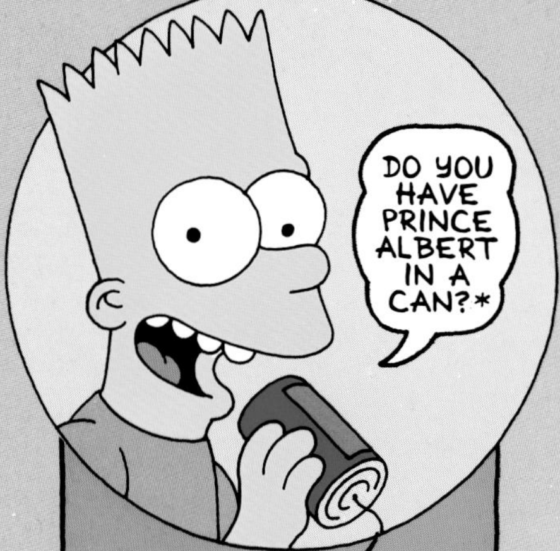
DO YOU HAVE PRINCE ALBERT IN A CAN?*

WACKY TALKY TIN CANS

TAKE 2 EMPTY, CLEAN TIN CANS WITH ONE END CUT OUT. PUNCH A SMALL HOLE IN EACH BOTTOM. POKE ONE END OF A 20-FOOT LENGTH OF HEAVY COTTON STRING THROUGH EACH OF THE HOLES. TIE KNOTS IN THE ENDS TO KEEP THE STRING FROM PULLING THROUGH. YOU AND A FRIEND STAND FAR ENOUGH APART THAT THE STRING IS PULLED TIGHT. NOW TALK INTO ONE CAN WHILE YOUR FRIEND LISTENS AT THE OTHER END!

*ASK YOUR GRANDPA WHAT THIS MEANS.

Madame Lisa's

MYSTICAL FORTUNE TELLER

Start with an 8 1/2" square piece of paper. Fold it in half diagonally both ways to find the center point (Fig. 1). Open up and fold each corner in to the center point (Fig. 2). Turn over and fold each corner of the smaller square in to the middle. Under each of these flaps, write an "answer": "Yeah, Man!," "No Way, Man! ," "Mmmaybe" and "Try Again." Or make up something. Write numbers on each of the flaps as shown (Fig. 3). Turn it over again and write numbers in each of the small triangular areas on that side (Fig. 4). Once again, turn it over. Now fold down the middle both ways to crease it. Push all four corners together and hold from the underside with the forefinger and thumb of each hand (Fig. 5). Your Mystical Fortune Teller is complete! Now have your friend ask a yes or no question and pick one of the numbers on the outside. Pull with the thumb and forefinger of one hand to open the center. Close it, then pull with the other two fingers to open the other way (Fig. 6). Go back and forth the number of times your friend picked. When you come to a stop ask him or her to pick one of the inside numbers and repeat the process. Finally, ask him or her to pick one more number. Open up the Fortune Teller and read the answer under that triangle.

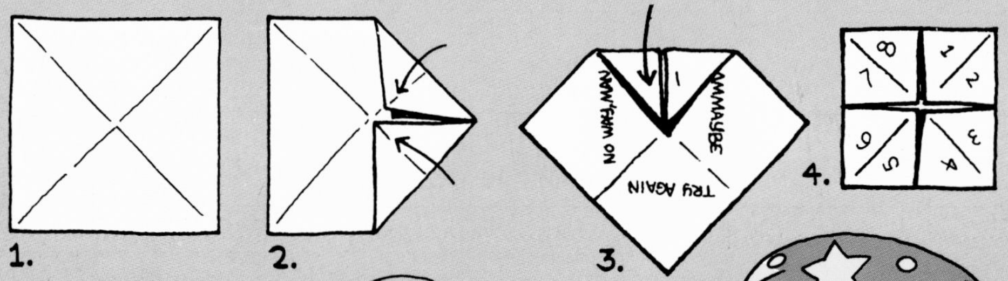
NO WAY, MAN!
MMMAYBE
TRY AGAIN
1.
2.
3.
4.

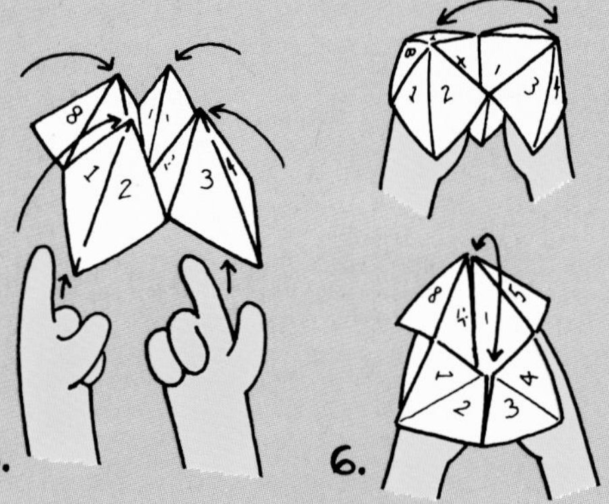
5.
6.

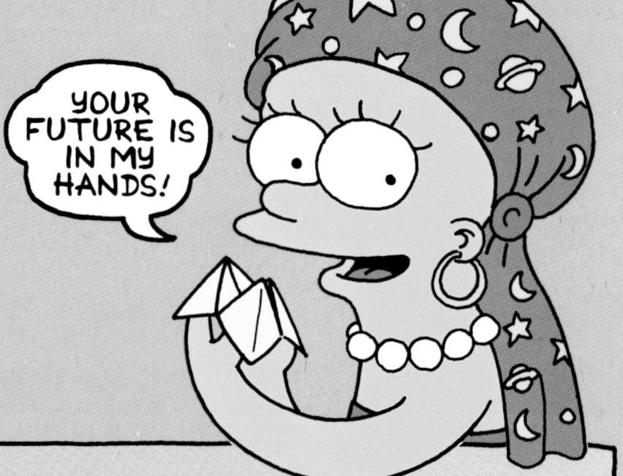
YOUR FUTURE IS IN MY HANDS!

HUMAN SARDINES

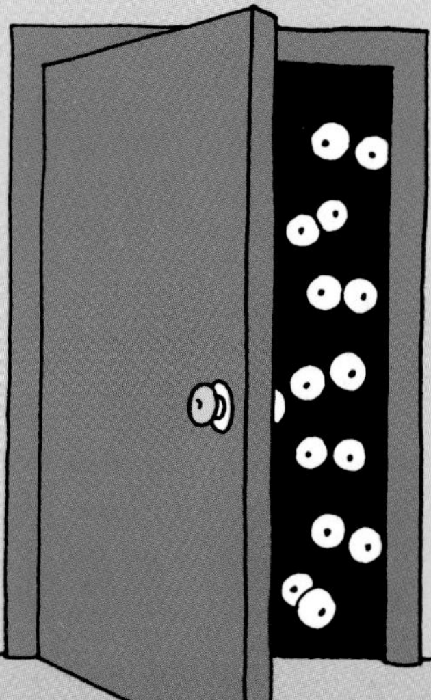

One person hides, in a place with a little extra room -- an out-of-the-way closet or under a bed or table covered with a cloth. Everyone else searches for him or her. When someone finds the hiding place, he or she gets in too. One by one, the players disappear...until only one is left, the loser.

SOLUTION ON PAGE 62.

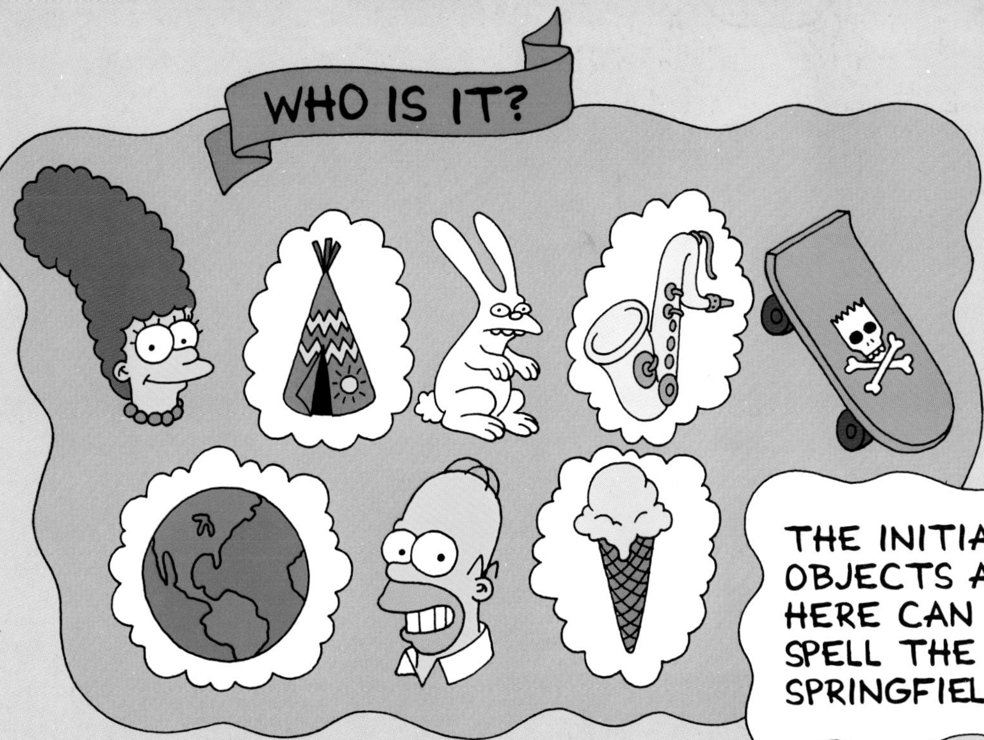
WHO IS IT?

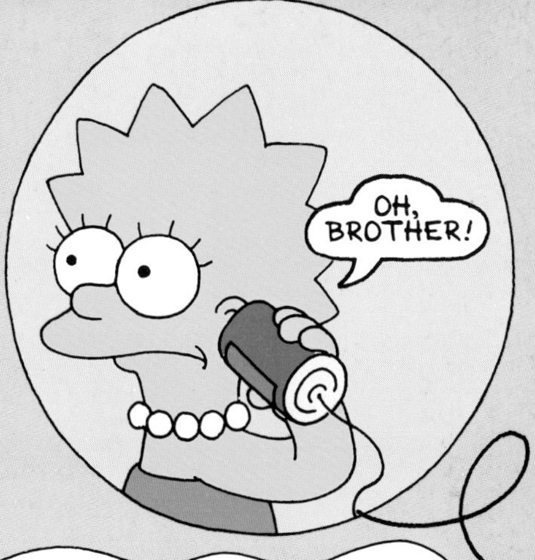
OH, BROTHER!

THE INITIAL LETTERS OF THE OBJECTS AND PEOPLE PICTURED HERE CAN BE ARRANGED TO SPELL THE NAME OF A CERTAIN SPRINGFIELD CITIZEN.

ADMIRAL BART'S BATTLESHIP

A game for two. Each player draws two big squares on a piece of paper. Then draw nine lines across and down, like in the picture below. Write 1 through 10 along the top of each and A through J down the side. One big square is the Battle Area, the other is the Target Area. Without showing each other where, draw ten battleships on the Battle Area. Five ships cover two squares each and five cover one square each. Leave at least one square between ships.

Keep your papers hidden from each other throughout the game. Each player takes a turn being the attacker by calling out a number and a letter (like A6). If the other player has a whole ship on that square, he or she says "direct hit." The attacker marks a B on his or her Target Area. If part of a ship is on that square, the defender says "damaged." The attacker knows he or she has sunk only half a ship. If no ship is on the square, the attacker draws an X in the same square on his or her Target Area. Then the other player is the attacker. The winner is the first one to sink all the other player's battleships.

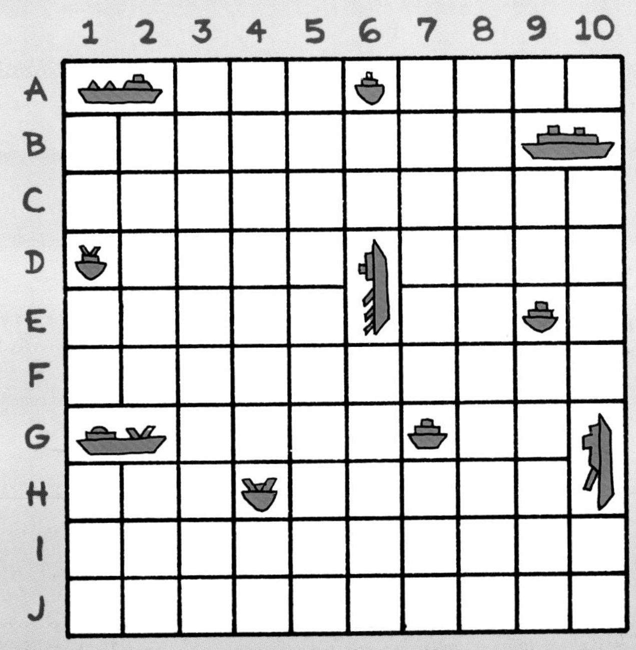
1 2 3 4 5 6 7 8 9 10
A B C D E F G H I J

BATTLE AREA

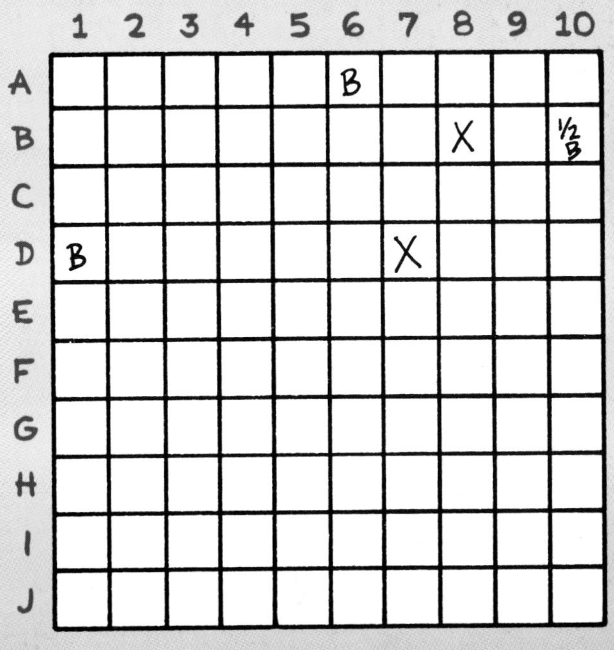
1 2 3 4 5 6 7 8 9 10
A B C D E F G H I J
B
X
1/2 B
B
X

TARGET AREA

Sideshow Bob's FLIPPED OUT FLIP BOOK

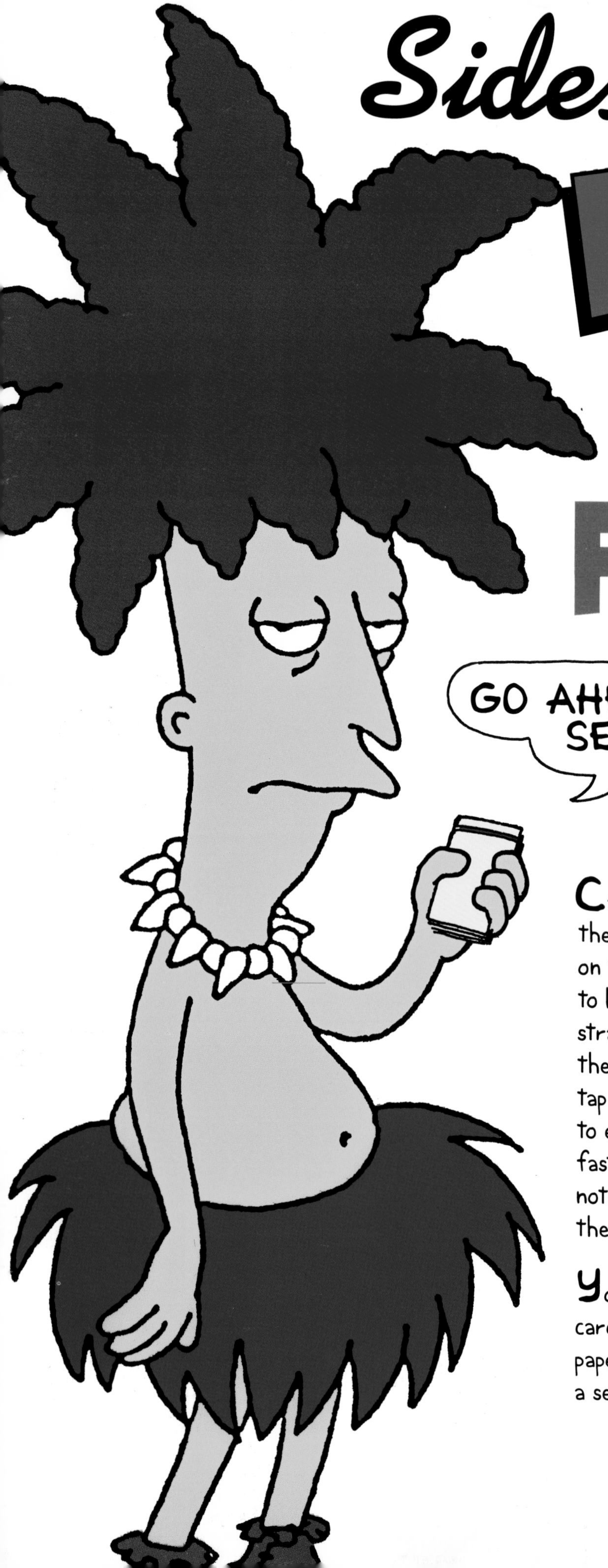
GO AHEAD AND FLIP IT. SEE IF I CARE.

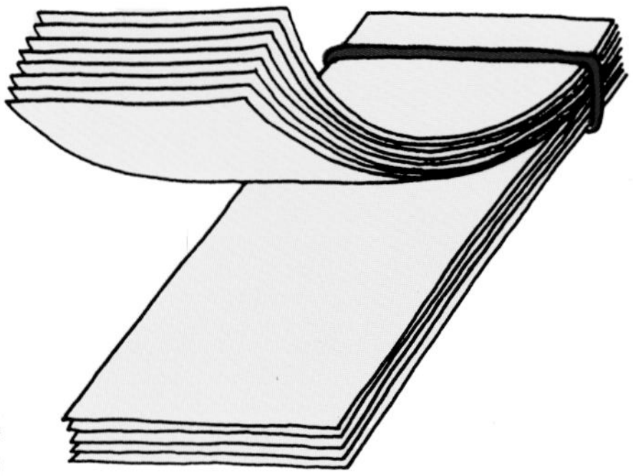

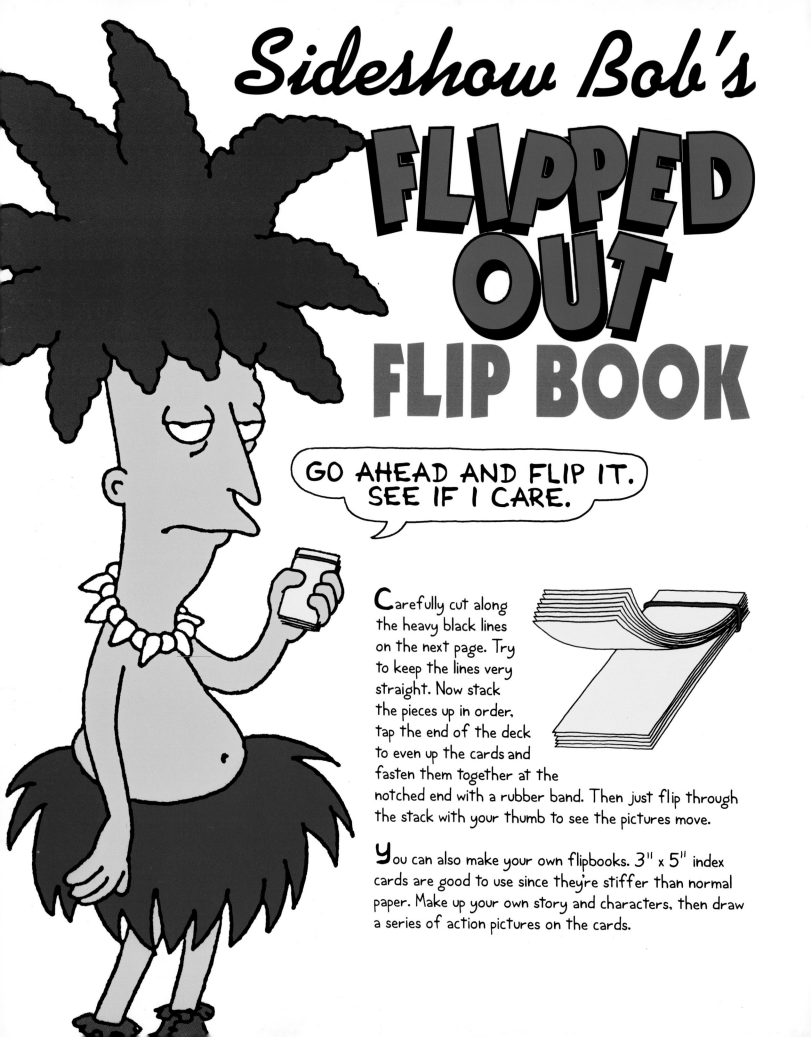

Carefully cut along the heavy black lines on the next page. Try to keep the lines very straight. Now stack the pieces up in order, tap the end of the deck to even up the cards and fasten them together at the notched end with a rubber band. Then just flip through the stack with your thumb to see the pictures move.

You can also make your own flipbooks. 3" x 5" index cards are good to use since they're stiffer than normal paper. Make up your own story and characters, then draw a series of action pictures on the cards.

CUT ALONG LINES.

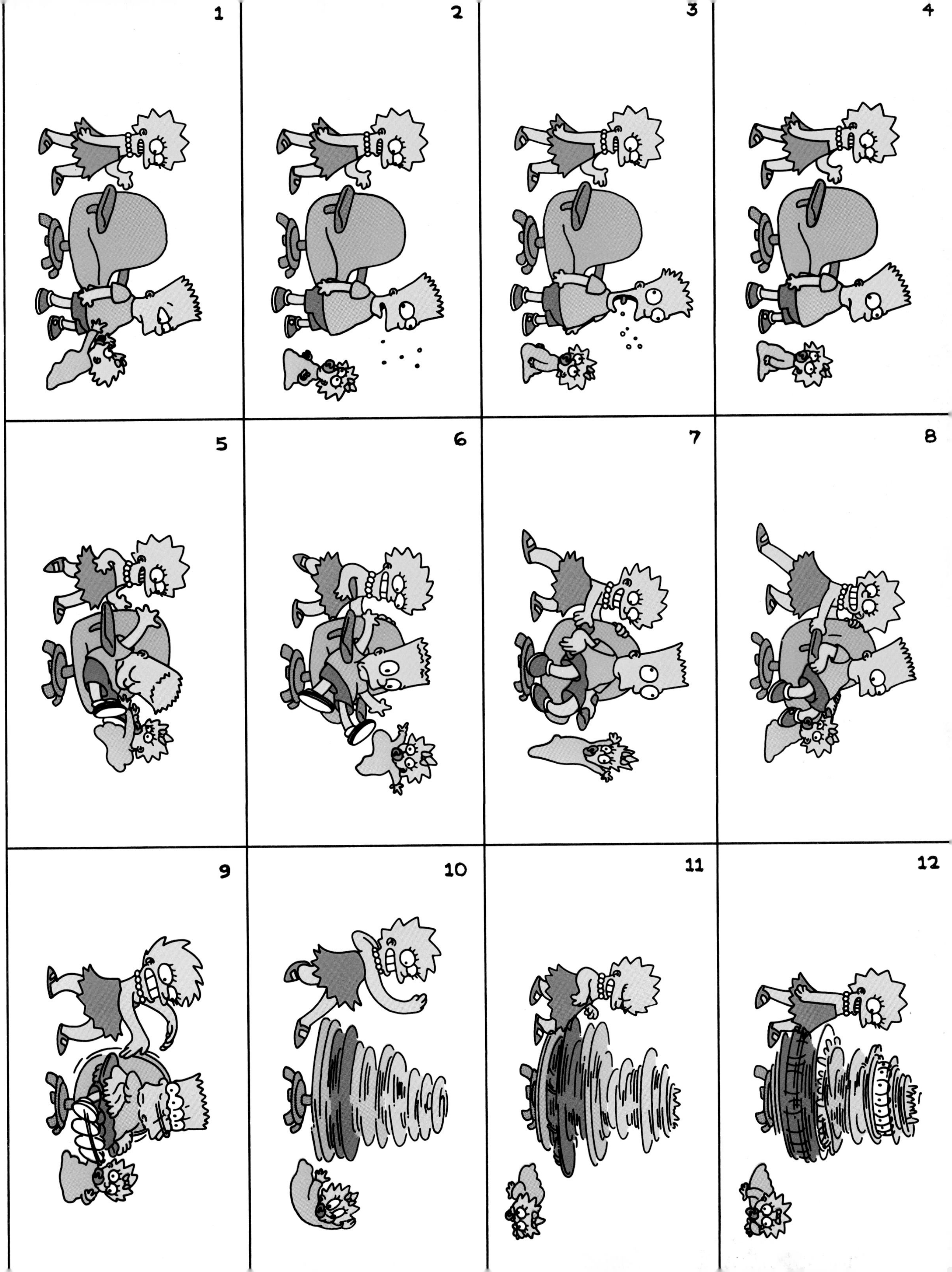
1
2
3
4
5
6
7
8
9
10
11
12

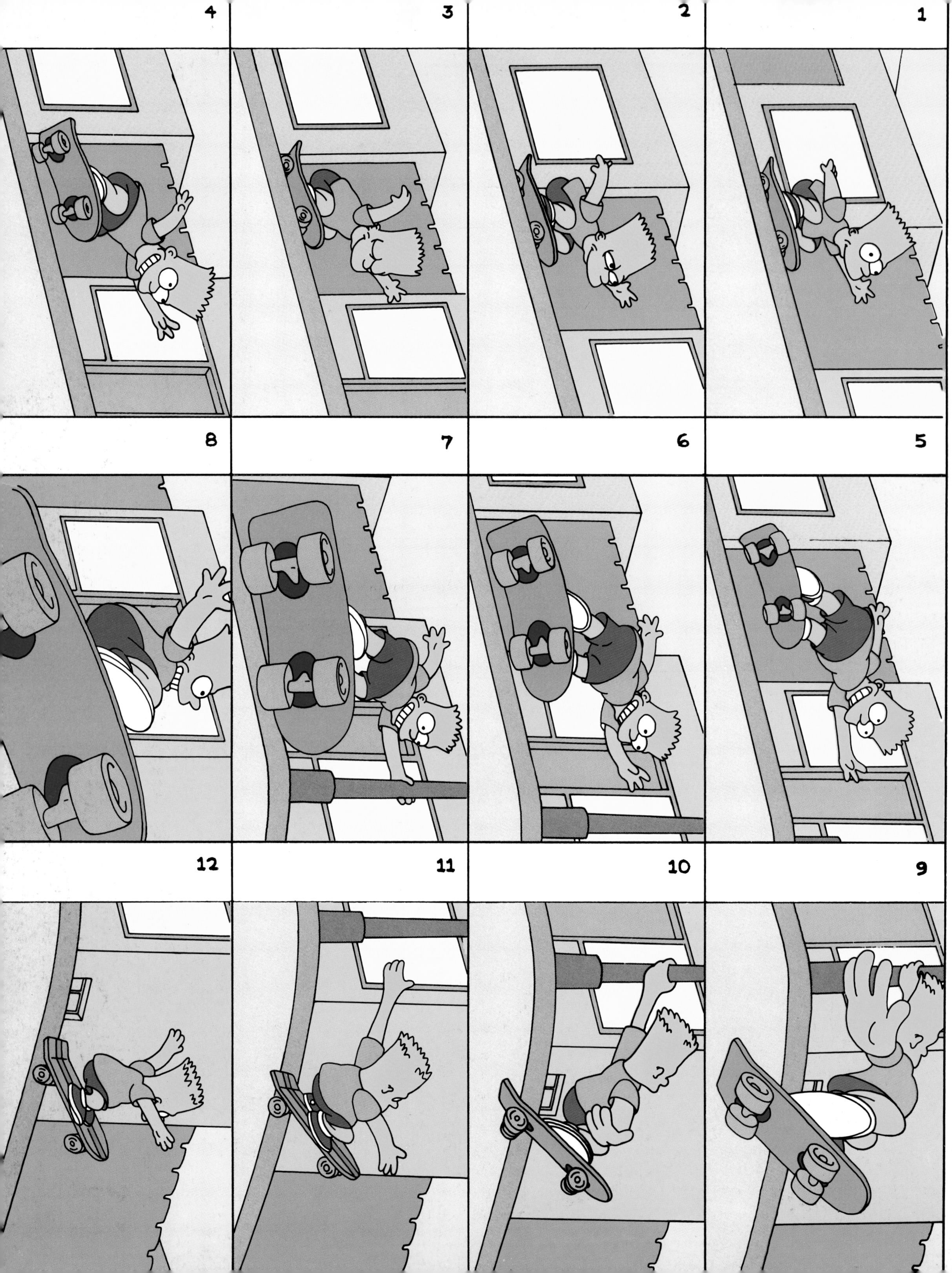

CUT ALONG LINES.

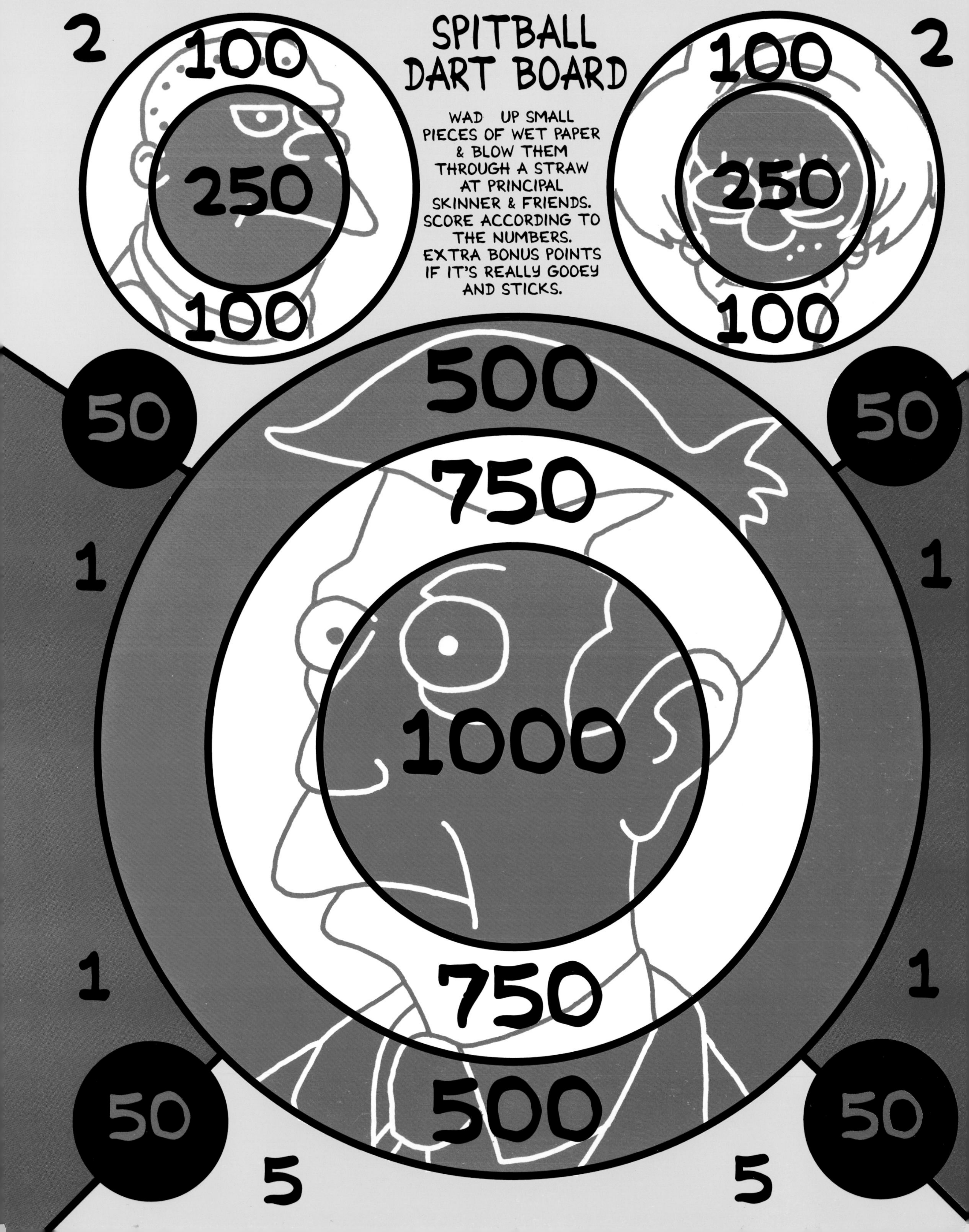
SPITBALL DART BOARD
WAD UP SMALL PIECES OF WET PAPER & BLOW THEM THROUGH A STRAW AT PRINCIPAL SKINNER & FRIENDS. SCORE ACCORDING TO THE NUMBERS. EXTRA BONUS POINTS IF IT'S REALLY GOOEY AND STICKS.
2
100
250
100
2
100
250
100
50
50
500
750
1
1000
1
1
750
1
500
50
50
5
5

Marge's WEEK-AT-A-GLANCE

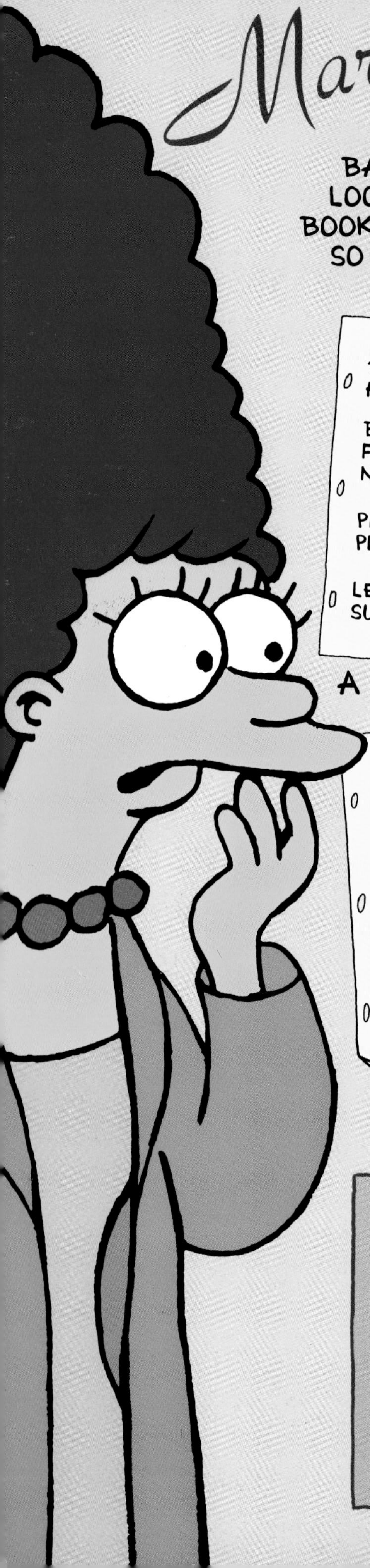

BART WENT RUMMAGING THROUGH MARGE'S PURSE LOOKING FOR LOOSE CHANGE AND HE GOT HER DATE BOOK ALL MIXED UP. CAN YOU REARRANGE THESE PAGES SO THEY ARE IN THE RIGHT CHRONOLOGICAL ORDER?

A

2PM - GET HAIRDO DONE

BUY GELATIN MIX FOR TOMORROW NIGHT'S DINNER

PICK UP PLACE MATS

LET THE SUNSHINE IN ☺

B

THROW OUT RECIPE FOR TOFU CUPCAKES

DISCUSS APPROPRIATE PUNISHMENT FOR BART WITH HOMER

TAKE MAGGIE TO VISIT HAMSTER FARM

PICK UP HOMER'S NEW BOWLING BALL

THINK POSITIVE THOUGHTS

C

MAIL ANGRY LETTER

GET FILM FOR TRIP TO HAMSTER FARM

1:30 MEET WITH BART'S PRINCIPAL

TRY OUT NEW RECIPE FOR TOFU CUPCAKES

INVITE PATTY & SELMA FOR LUNCH DAY AFTER TOMORROW

D

TAKE TIME TO SMELL THE ROSES

VACUUM HEAVY FOOT TRAFFIC LANES

PREPARE TASTY GELATIN DESSERT

8PM - MR. BURNS FOR DINNER!!!

E

CALL BETTY'S BEAUTY BARN FOR APPOINTMENT

WRITE ANGRY LETTER TO THE EDITOR ABOUT THOSE DARN NOISY LEAF-BLOWERS!

ORGANIZE HOMER'S SOCK DRAWER

(HAVE A NICE DAY)

F

DROP OFF HAMSTER FILM FOR DEVELOPING

ORDER SPECIAL VINYL PLACE MATS FOR HOMER'S BOSS'S DINNER

PATTY & SELMA FOR LUNCH

BART GROUNDED

7PM - BOWLING

MARGE'S HAIRDO SECRET REBUSLY REVEALED

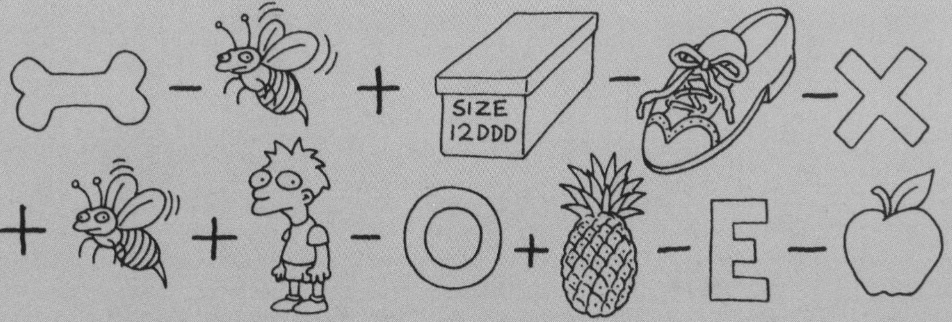

SIZE 12DDD

Answers on Page 62.

Otto's WILD RIDE!

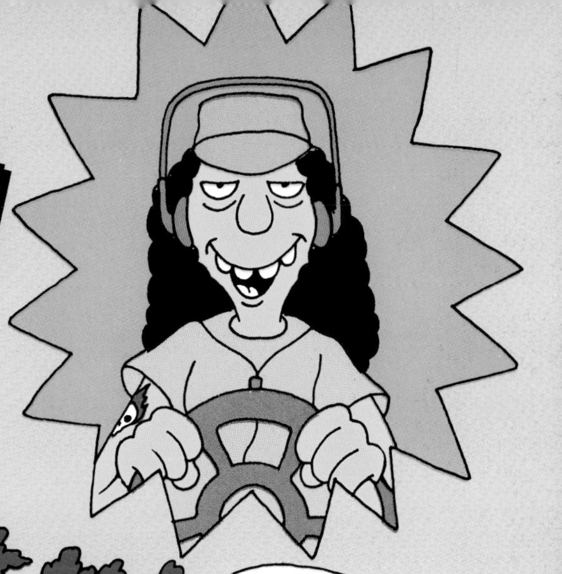

FAR OUT, MAN! OTTO'S GOT A BUSLOAD OF EAGER CHILDREN WHO CAN'T WAIT TO GET TO SCHOOL! IF YOU CAN BELIEVE THIS, HELP OTTO FIND THE QUICKEST ROUTE TO SCHOOL.

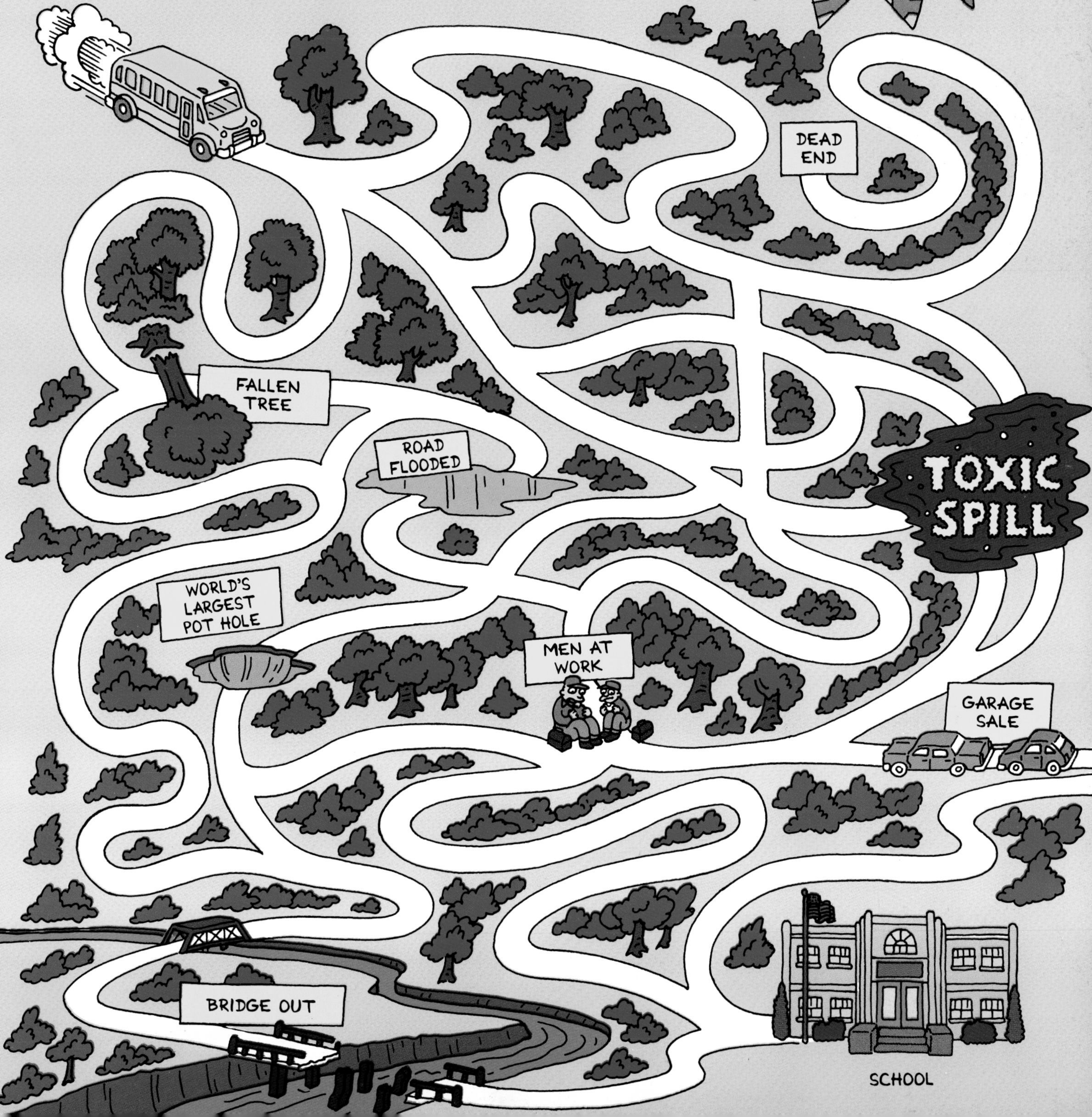
DEAD END
FALLEN TREE
ROAD FLOODED
TOXIC SPILL
WORLD'S LARGEST POT HOLE
MEN AT WORK
GARAGE SALE
BRIDGE OUT
SCHOOL

SOLUTION ON PAGE 62.

Lights Out! It's Time for HANDY SHADOW SHOWS

TURN OFF ALL THE LIGHTS EXCEPT ONE LAMP. POSITION THE LAMP SO THAT IT SHINES ON A BLANK WALL. YOUR HANDS SHOULD BE ABOUT 3 FEET FROM THE LIGHT AND ABOUT 4 FEET FROM THE WALL. THE NEARER YOUR HANDS ARE TO THE LIGHT, THE LARGER AND LESS DISTINCT THE SHADOW WILL BE ON THE WALL. NOW, ARRANGE YOUR HANDS AND FINGERS IN THE POSITIONS SHOWN TO MAKE THESE FIGURES.

Like This!

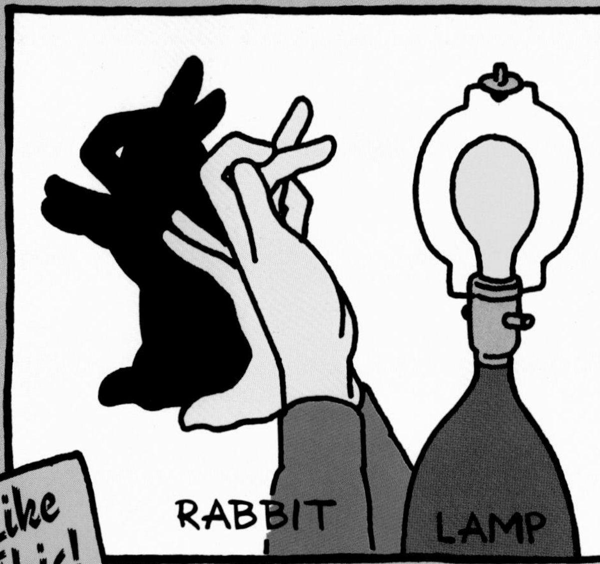
RABBIT
LAMP

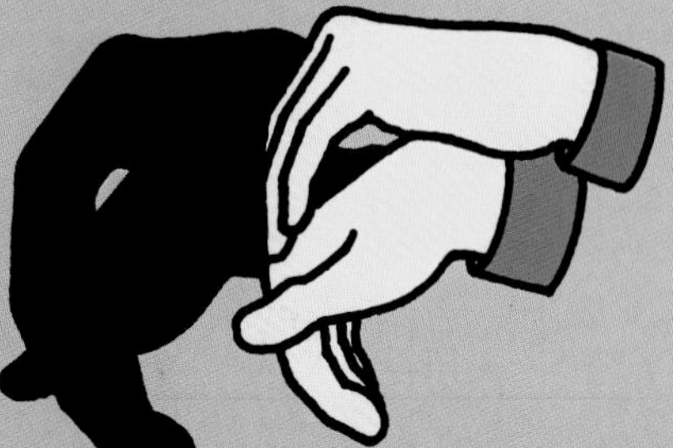

RAMPAGING ELEPHANT

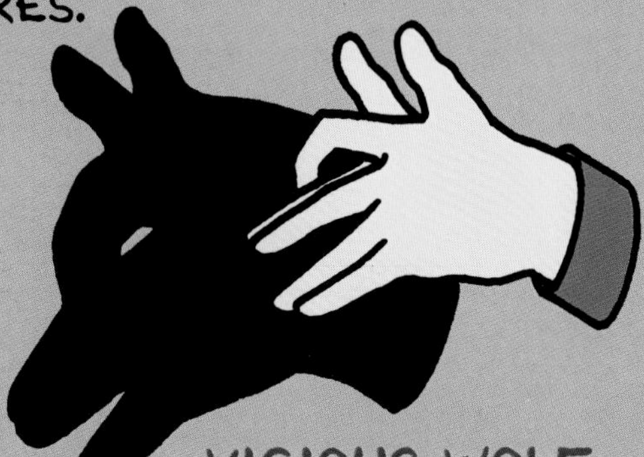

VICIOUS WOLF

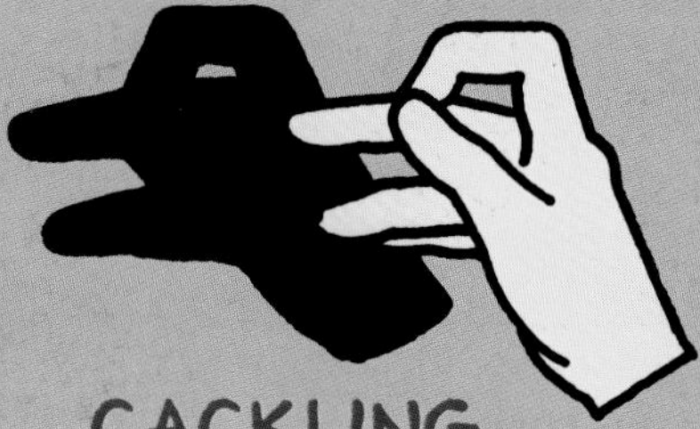

CACKLING GOOSE

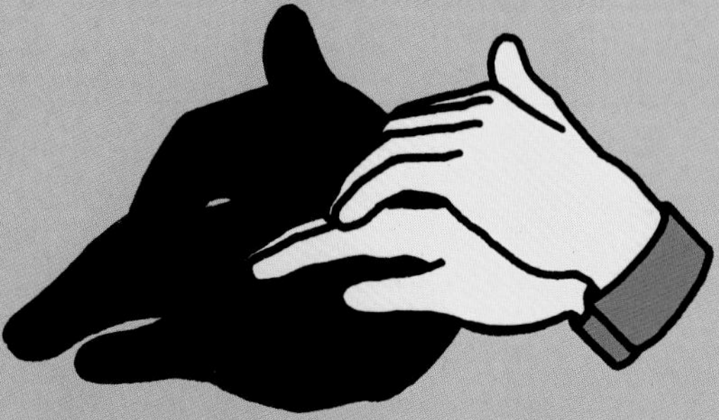

PECULIAR PIG

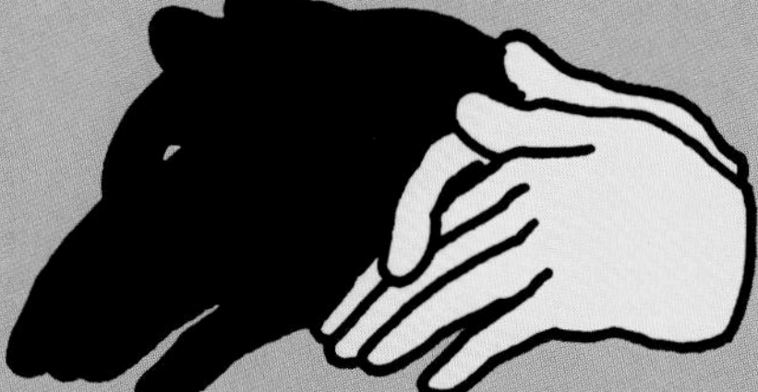

RABID BEAR

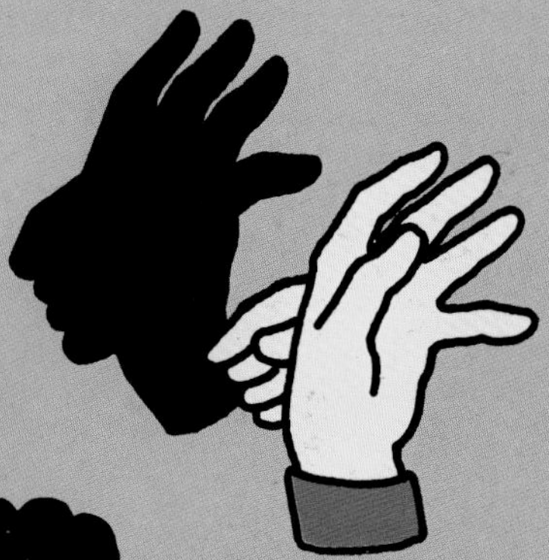

FUNKY REGGAE SINGER

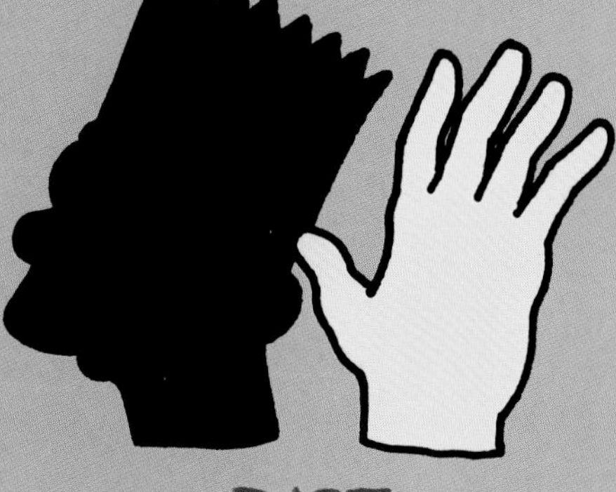

BART

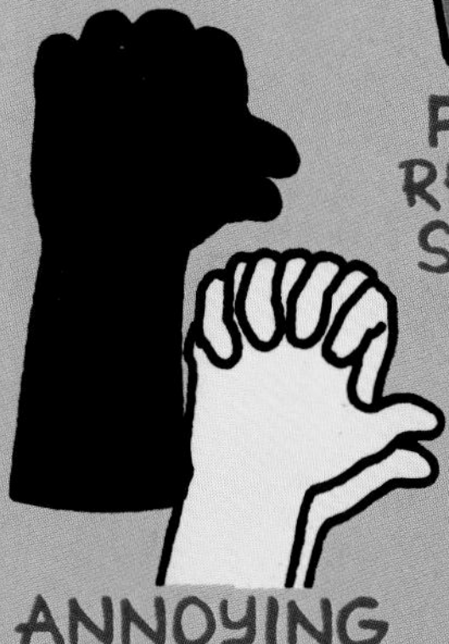

ANNOYING ROOSTER

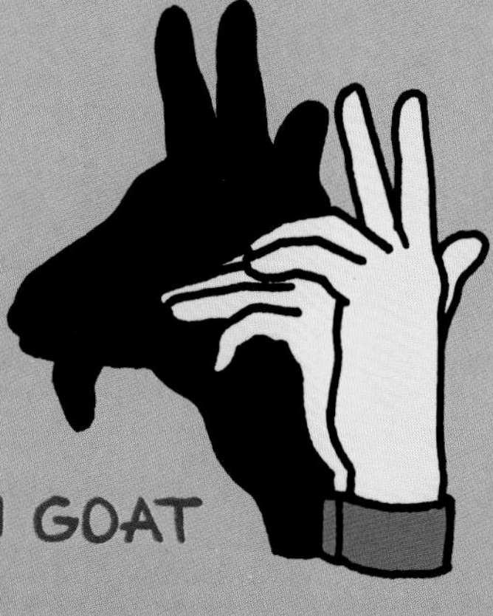

PESKY GOAT

TRY TO CREATE OTHER SHADOW PICTURES!

Spinning Spiral Thingy

CUT OUT OR COPY THE SPIRAL. BE CAREFUL TO FOLLOW THE LINES. MAKE A SMALL DENT IN THE PAPER WHERE THE DOT IS SO IT WON'T SLIP OFF THE POINT, THEN BALANCE IT ON A PENCIL AS SHOWN. NOW HOLD IT OVER A LIGHTED ELECTRIC BULB AND WATCH IT SPIN!

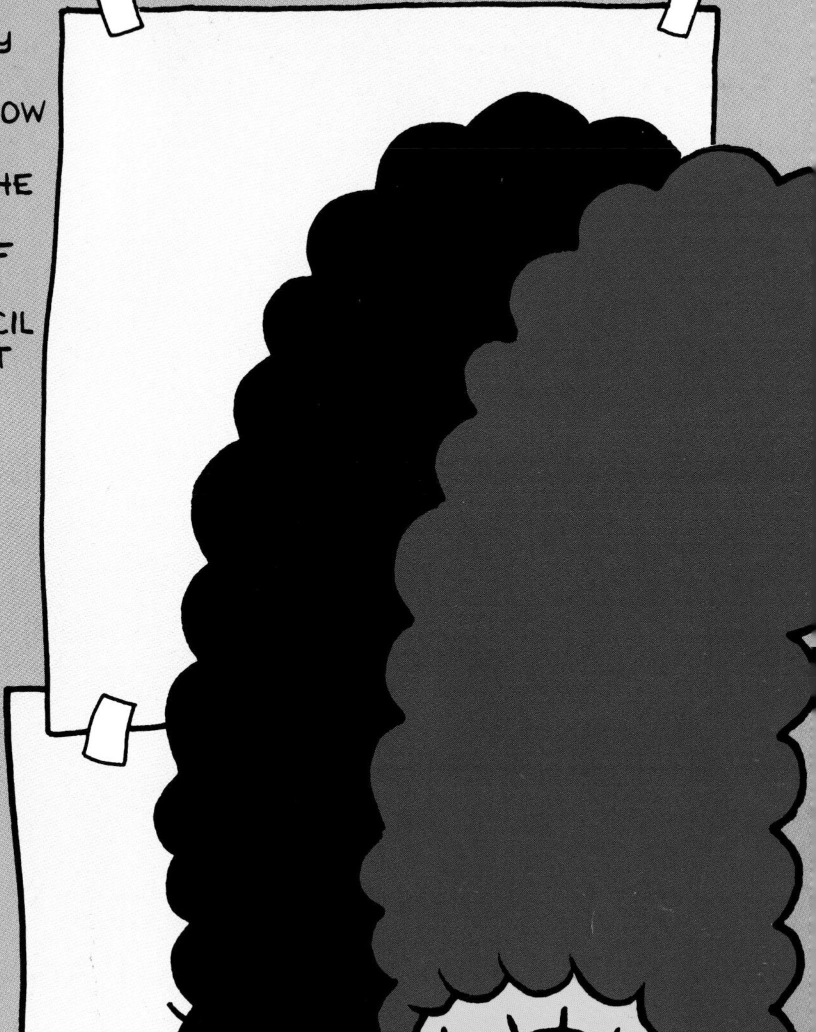

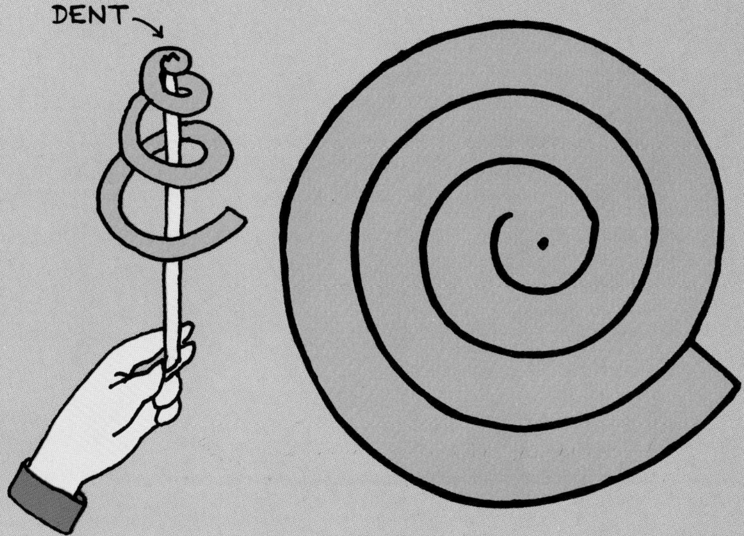
DENT

Silly Shady SILHOUETTES

YOU CAN ALSO USE THE LAMP TO DRAW A SILHOUETTE. TAPE A PIECE OF PAPER TO THE WALL WHERE THE SHADOWS ARE CAST. NOW, HAVE YOUR FRIEND POSITION HERSELF SO THAT HER PROFILE CASTS A SHADOW ON THE PAPER. BY TRACING AROUND HER SHADOW, YOU DRAW A SILHOUETTE.

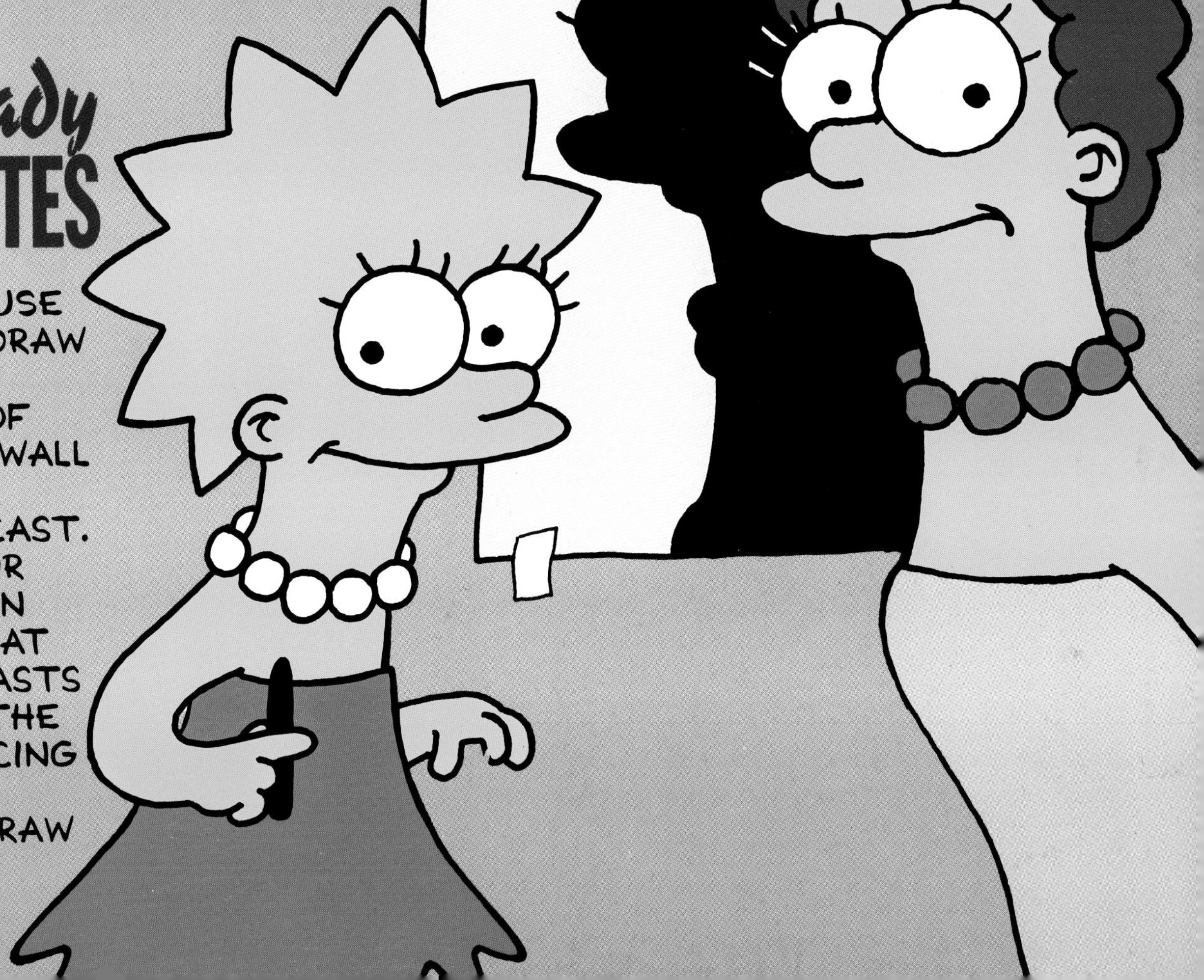

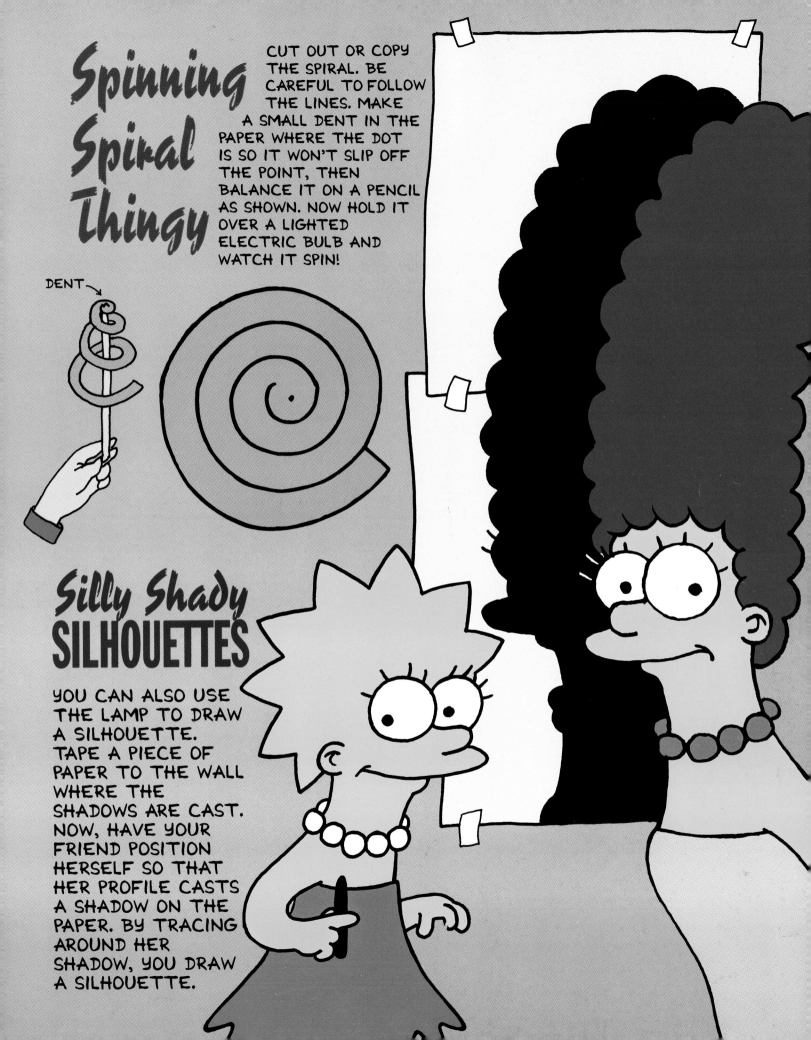

PAPER-MANIA

WHOA, MAMA!!!
LOOKS LIKE THAT ONE GOT TOO CLOSE TO THE NUCLEAR POWER PLANT!

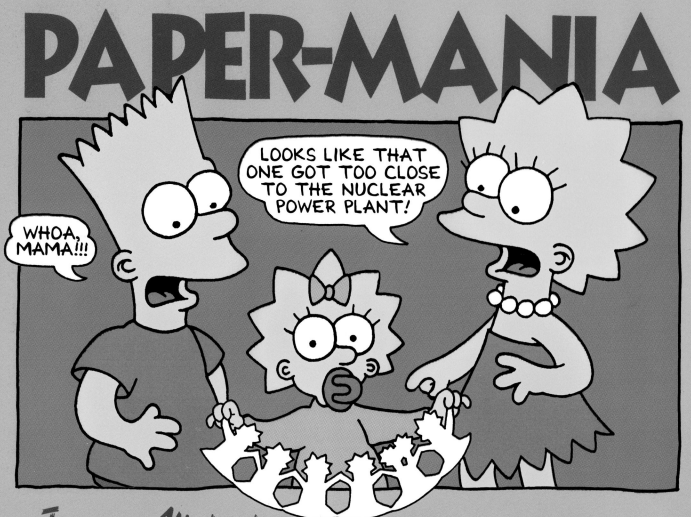

Teenage Mutant PAPERDOLLS

You'll need a strip of paper 2" to 4" wide and 24" to 27" long. You can make it by cutting several sheets of paper lengthwise and sticking them together with clear tape. Fold the strip into eight or nine 3" accordion folds, but have one of the folds go only about half way, as in Fig. A. Make this fold the second or third fold. The dotted lines in Figs. B, C. and D indicate the edge of the half fold. Make the first cut (No. 1), almost to this edge. Follow Fig. C and D to finish the cutout. It will look like Fig. E when it's unfolded.

A.
B.
C.
D.
E.

THE BAFFLING MOBIUS STRIP

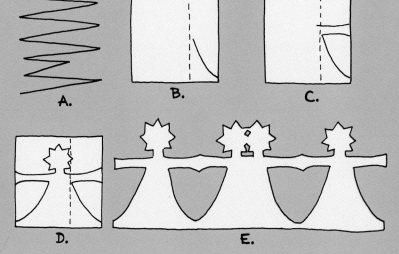

CUT OUT A STRIP OF PAPER AT LEAST 12 INCHES LONG AND ABOUT 2 INCHES WIDE. MAKE ONE TWIST IN IT, THEN TAPE THE TWO ENDS TOGETHER. TRY TO FIGURE OUT WHICH SIDE IS WHICH BY DRAWING A SINGLE LINE LENGTHWISE DOWN ONE SIDE. HAVING A LITTLE TROUBLE? NOW CUT ALONG THAT LINE, ALL THE WAY AROUND THE LENGTH OF THE STRIP. YOU THINK YOU'LL GET TWO CIRCLES NOW, RIGHT? HA! TRY IT AND SEE!

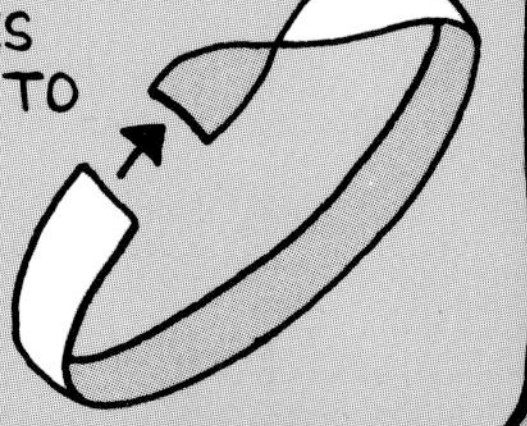

Loop-the-Loop Airplane

FOLD
FOLD
FOLD
1.
FOLD
A
2.
FOLD DOWN
3.
FOLD
FOLD
4.

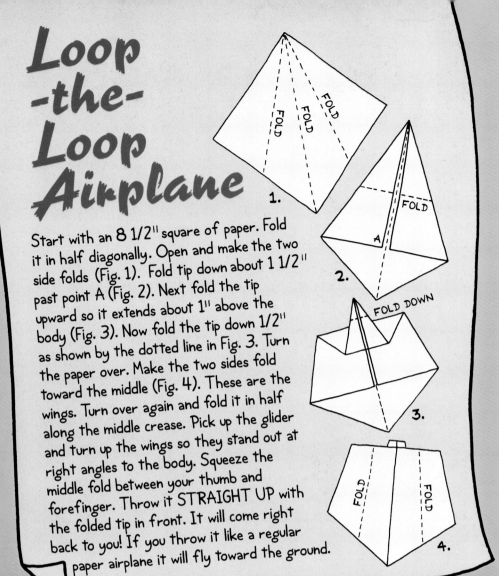

Start with an 8 1/2" square of paper. Fold it in half diagonally. Open and make the two side folds (Fig. 1). Fold tip down about 1 1/2" past point A (Fig. 2). Next fold the tip upward so it extends about 1" above the body (Fig. 3). Now fold the tip down 1/2" as shown by the dotted line in Fig. 3. Turn the paper over. Make the two sides fold toward the middle (Fig. 4). These are the wings. Turn over again and fold it in half along the middle crease. Pick up the glider and turn up the wings so they stand out at right angles to the body. Squeeze the middle fold between your thumb and forefinger. Throw it STRAIGHT UP with the folded tip in front. It will come right back to you! If you throw it like a regular paper airplane it will fly toward the ground.

THE BIG POPPER

1.
2.
3.
4.

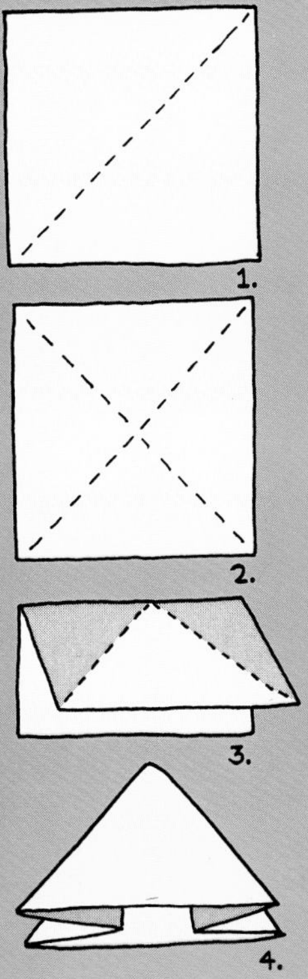

Take a big square sheet of newspaper. Fold diagonally corner to corner (Fig. 1). Open and fold the other corners the same way (Fig. 2). Open up and then fold in half (Fig. 3). Push in the shaded areas, making the folds sharp (Fig. 4). Hold with your pointer finger in between two of the points (Fig. 5) and snap your wrist down hard. The fold on the other side will snap out with a loud pop! Just tuck it back in to use again and again.

5.

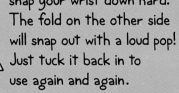

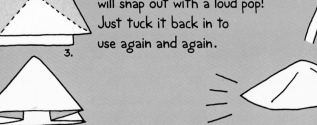

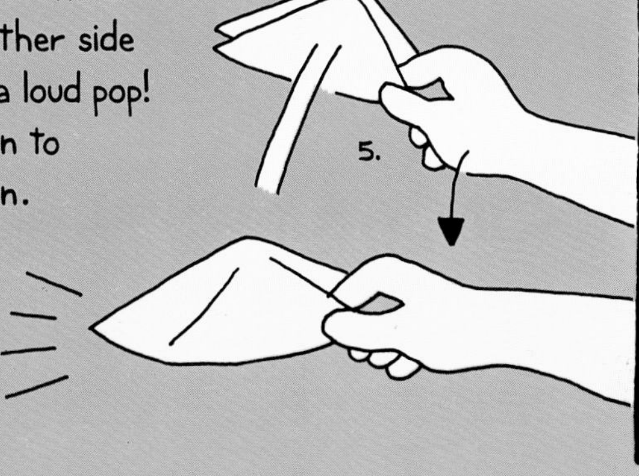

Gyrating GYROCOPTER

You can either use this one or copy it onto another piece of paper. Cut out along the heavy black lines. Don't cut along the dotted lines. Fold on lines A and B. Staple the sides together or wind some tape around them to keep them together. Now fold the blades along line C, bending one blade in one direction and the other blade in the opposite direction. Stand on some high place, hold by the bottom with the blades spread out and let go!

C
A
B

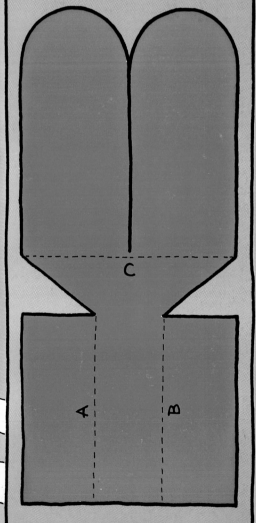

MESSIN' UP THE KITCHEN!

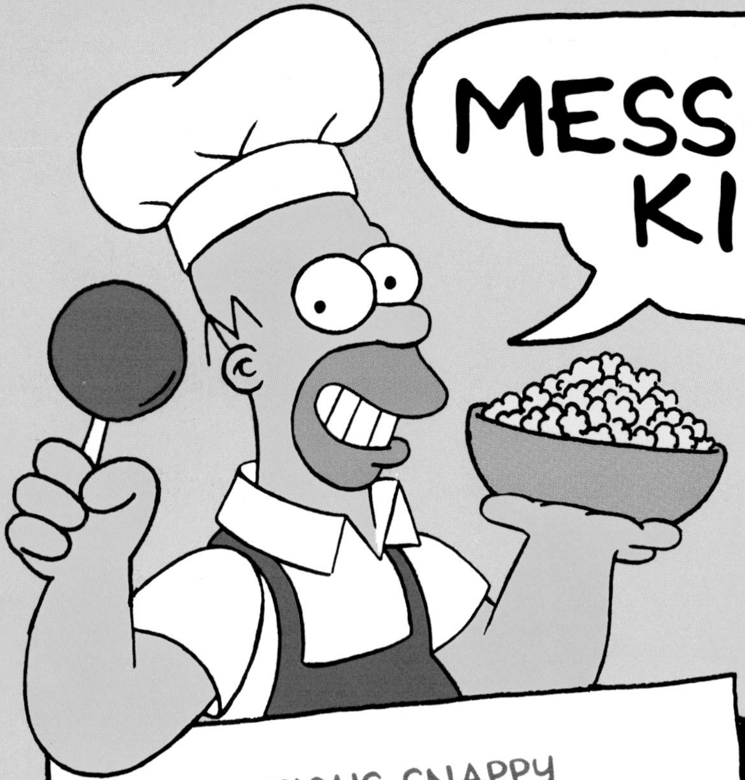

ICKY STICKS

(Not that kind. The kind you eat!)

Boil rapidly 2 cups of sugar, 2/3 cup of white corn syrup and 1/2 cup of water. It's done when you drop a small amount of the goop into a glass of cold water and it turns brittle. Remove from the range and stir in your favorite flavoring extract and food coloring. Drop by tablespoonfuls onto a greased cookie sheet and press a plastic spoon or fork into each one. They'll harden on the counter for consumption in an hour or so.

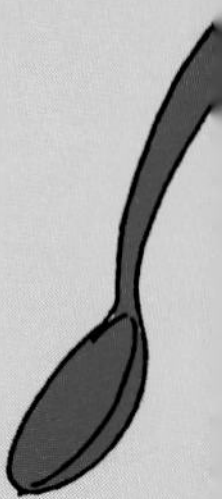

SCRUMPTIOUS SNAPPY POPCORN TOPPERS

Melt a little butter or margarine together with one of the following, and toss it into your next batch of freshly microwaved popcorn:

1/4 Teaspoon garlic powder (STINKY corn)
1/4 Cup shredded cheese (SLIMY corn)
1 Tablespoon peanut butter (STICKY corn)
2 Tablespoons brown sugar and a dash of cinnamon (SWEETY corn)
1/2 Teaspoon curry powder (SASSY corn)
1/2 Teaspoon chili powder (SPICY corn)

COWS HAVE FOUR STOMACHS.

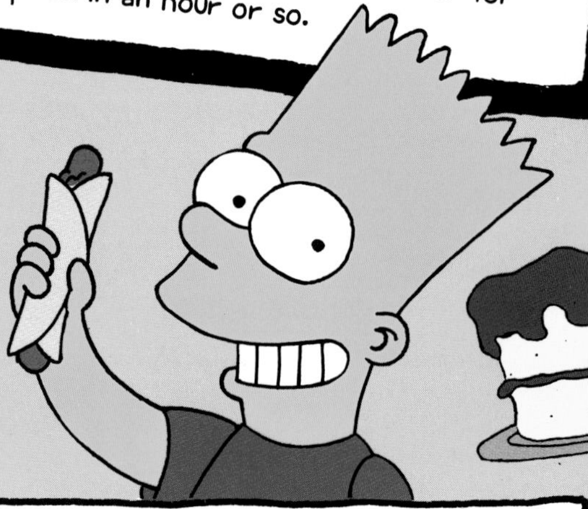

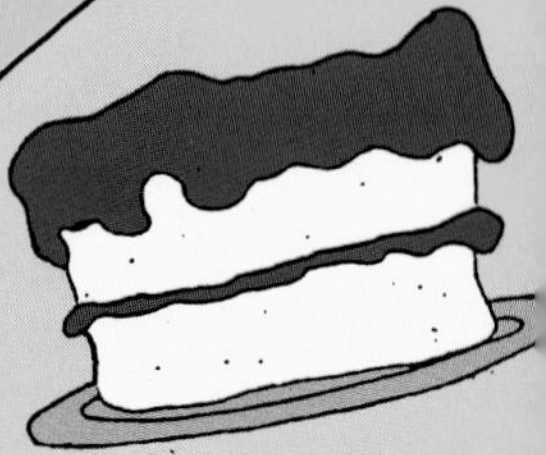

BART'S DOG-URRITOS

Boil one hotdog. Open one can of chili and heat it up in a pan. Grate up a little American cheese (or processed cheese food, for that ol' fashioned additive flavor). Wrap the dog, some chili and the cheese in a flour tortilla. Presto!

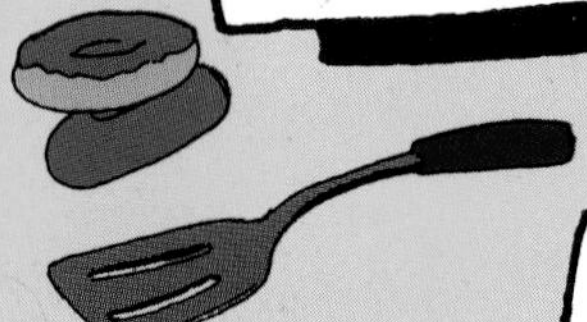

IF YOU HOLD YOUR NOSE WHILE YOU EAT, YOU WON'T TASTE YOUR FOOD.

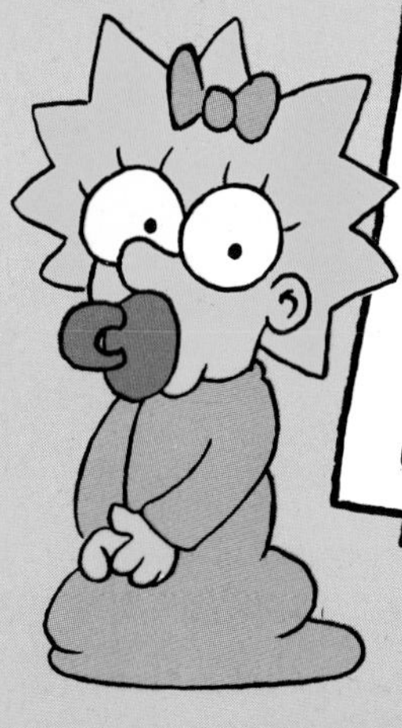

MAGGIE'S MUDPIES

One Cup dirt
1/2 Cup water
Tasty additions: small pebbles, dried leaves, bugs, plastic toys, worms.

Mix thoroughly. Shape into pies (or cupcakes). Bake on a hot sidewalk for 15 minutes. Eat. Or wear!

INSTANT PEANUT BUTTER BALLS

Mash together in a large bowl: 1 cup crunchy peanut butter and 1/2 cup dry milk powder and 1 cup shredded coconut and 1 teaspoon vanilla extract and 1 cup chopped dates or raisins. Roll the delectable mess into bite-sized balls, coat with sesame seeds and pop into your mouth. If you can manage not to eat them all, store the leftovers in the fridge.

BLENDERIZED DELECTABLE GUZZLERS

Whiz around for about 15 seconds:

A Cup of yogurt + a Cup of any fruit juice + a handful of ice cubes

Half a banana (in chunks) + a Cup of orange juice + a dash of ginger

A Cup of yogurt + a Cup of fruit, fresh or frozen or even canned. Add a little cinnamon for spice.

A Cup of milk + a Tablespoon each of cocoa powder and of sugar or honey + a dash each of vanilla extract and cinnamon + a handful of ice cubes

A Scoop of ice cream + 1/2 Cup milk + a half banana, chunked + two dashes of cocoa powder and some cinnamon

HAND-MASHED SANDWICH SPREADS

Mash by hand:
1/2 Cup peanut butter + 1 large banana and a dash of cinnamon and/or coconut + a fingerful of raisins
    OR
1/2 Cup peanut butter + 1/2 Cup softened cream cheese + a little honey + a few raisins

SUGARY SUGAR COOKIES

Turn on oven and make sure you have the following yum-licious ingredients:

400°

3/4 Cup butter or margarine. Use butter for a buttery taste. Use margarine for a sort of buttery taste.

1 Teaspoon vanilla... the extracted kind.

1 Cup pure white fallen sugar granules.

3/4 Cup of all-purpose flour after major nutrients have been taken out and put back in again.

2 eggs from either ranch-fed or chemically injected chickens. There's no taste difference anyway.

1 Teaspoon each baking powder and salt. (Use salt substitute if you're worried.)

☆ ⊂ ★ ☆ OKAY, WE CAN BEGIN ☆ ⊂ ★

In a large bowl of an electric mixer, beat butter and sugar until creamy, then beat in eggs and vanilla. In another bowl, stir together flour, baking powder and salt; gradually add this to butter mixture, blending thoroughly, to form a soft dough. Cover tightly with plastic wrap and refrigerate until firm (at least 1 hour or for up to 3 days).

On a floured board, roll out dough, a portion at a time, to a thickness of 1/8 inch (keep remaining portions refrigerated). Cut out with cookie cutters (about 2 1/2 inches in diameter) and place slightly apart on ungreased baking sheets. Sprinkle generously with sugar.

Bake at 400° in the oven for 8 to 10 minutes or until edges are lightly browned. Transfer to racks and let cool completely before handling. Store airtight in a hiding place that kids don't know about. Makes about 4 dozen scrump-tastic cookies. Should last a few days in a normal household. At our house, they're gone in 20 minutes.

OPTIONAL For Marge's extra special "MULTICOLORED" cookies, just add a few drops of food coloring to each portion.

YOUR STOMACH IS THE SIZE OF A GRAPEFRUIT.

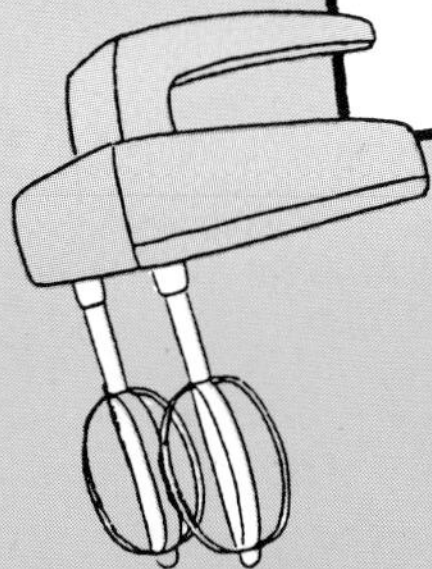

SOME-MORES
(Atomic Style)

Break off a piece of a chocolate bar and place it on a graham cracker and then put a marshmallow on top. Pop into the microwave, nuke 'em for a few seconds. Voila!

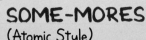

THE SIMPSONS'

HECK-OF-A-DECK OF CARD GAMES

OLD MAIDS

For 3 to 5 players. The object of this game is to get rid of all your cards and NOT to get stuck with the "OLD MAIDS" card. Deal out all the cards, using only one of the two "OLD MAIDS" cards. Everyone sets down any pairs in his or her hand face up on the table. The player on the dealer's left holds out his or her cards face-down to the player on his or her left, who picks a card. Then that player does the same to the next player. Anytime you get a pair, set it down on the table. When you're out of cards (all have been paired off), you're safely out of the game. Sooner or later, everyone will drop out except the one holding the "OLD MAIDS."

CONCENTRATION

Deal all the cards out on a table, face down, in rows or in any pattern you'd like. Players take turns at turning two cards at a time face up. Whenever they make a matching pair, you keepthem in your pile. If they don't match, you turn them face down again, and the next player tries. The winner is the person with the most cards when all of them have been removed from the table.

WAR

For 2 players. Deal out the whole deck face down in a pile in front of each player. Both players turn their top cards over at the same time. The one with the high card takes both and puts them under his stack. (In this game the ace is low and the king is high.) If the cards are the same value, "War" is declared. Each player turns up another card; the high card takes all four cards. If there's another tie, do it again until someone gets the high card. The winner is the one holding all the cards at the end.

SLAPBART

Use all the Bart/Joker cards. Deal all the cards out to the players, in face-down stacks. Everyone takes a turn turning over his or her top card into a center pile. When a Bart/Joker turns up, the first person to slap it with his or her hand wins all the cards in the center stack.

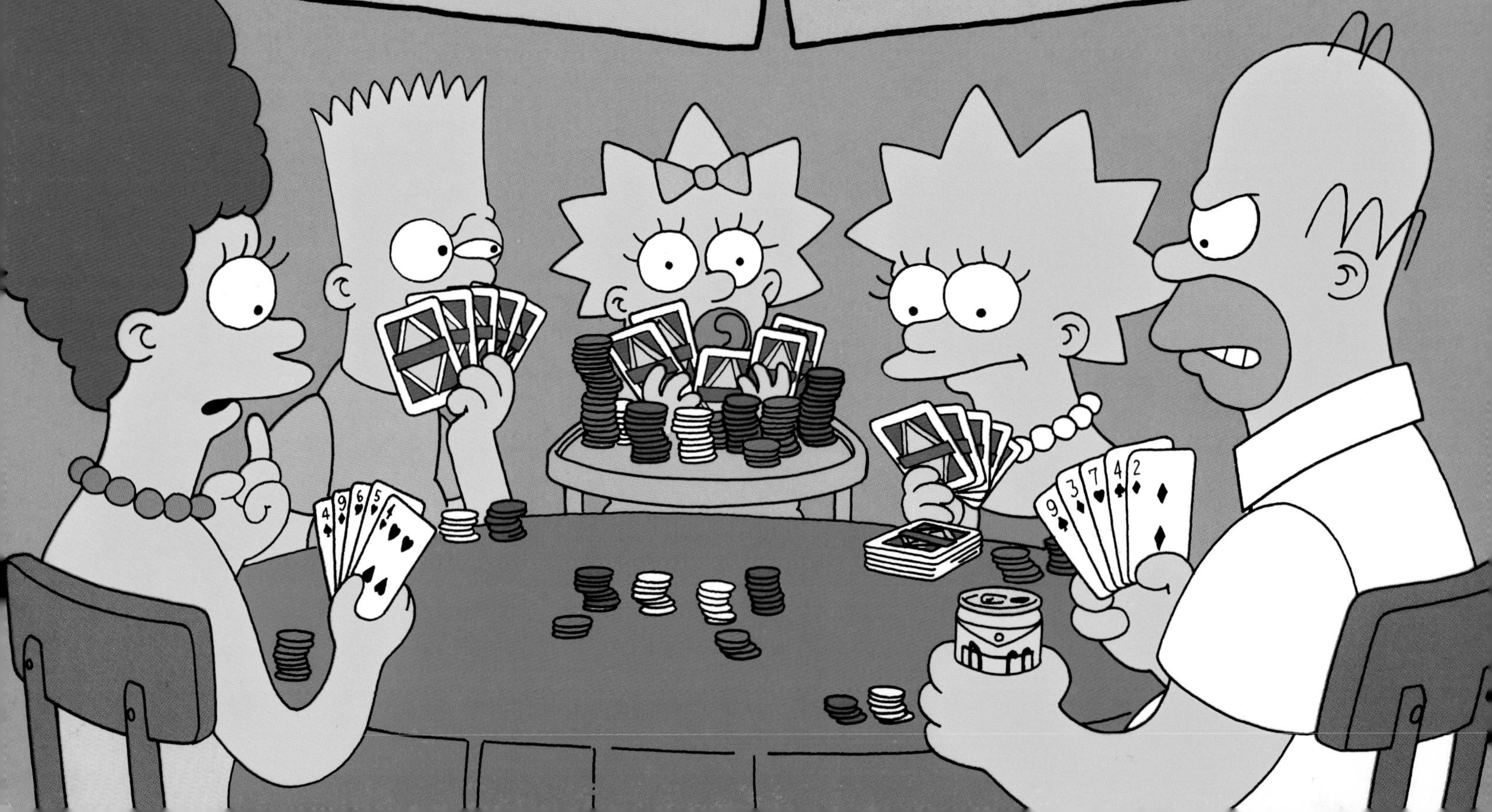

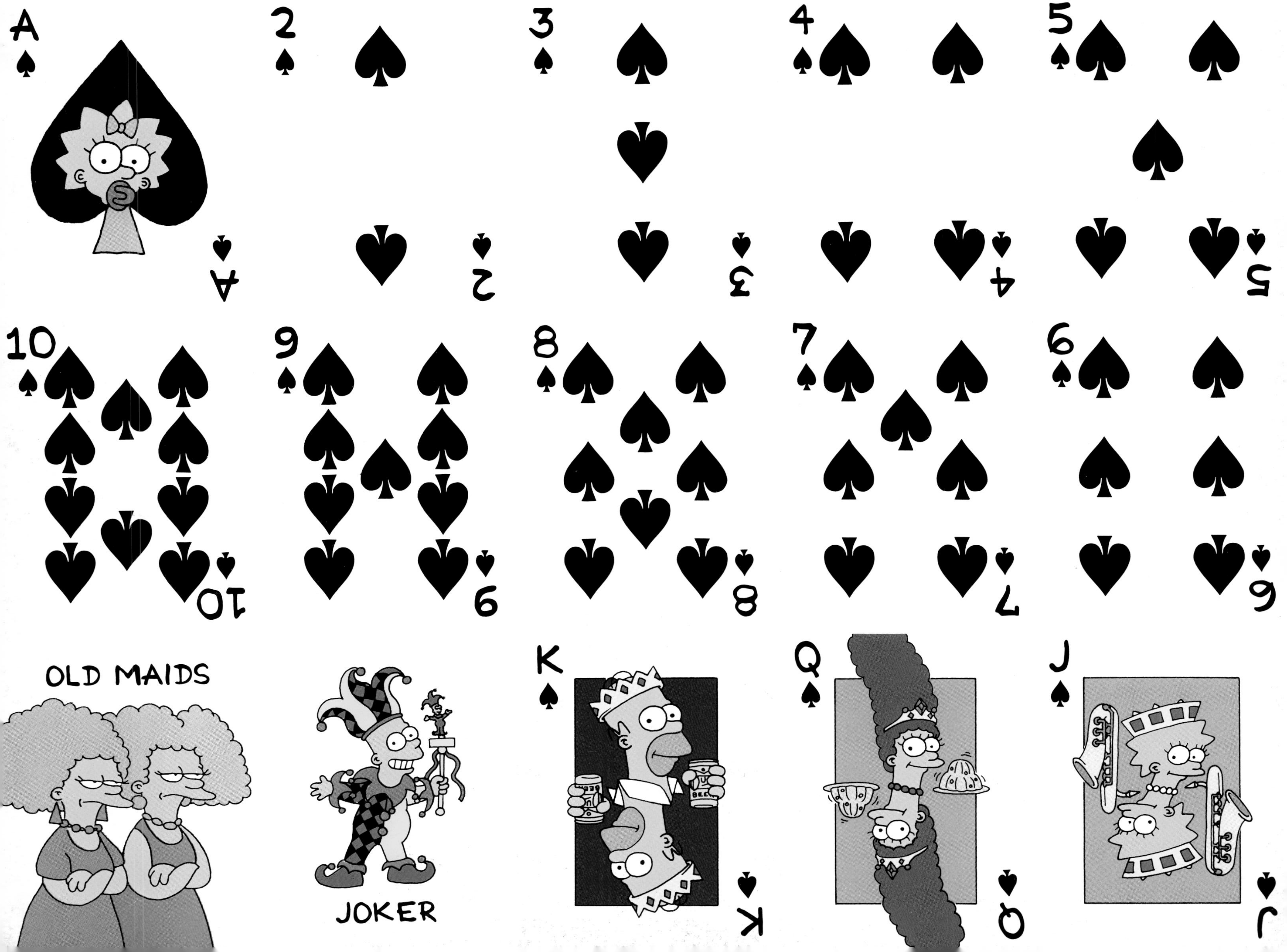
A
2
3
4
5
10
9
8
7
6
OLD MAIDS
JOKER
K
Q
J

CUT ALONG BLUE LINES AND PLAY!

OFFICIAL
HECK-OF-A-DECK
SIMPSONS™
PLAYING
CARDS

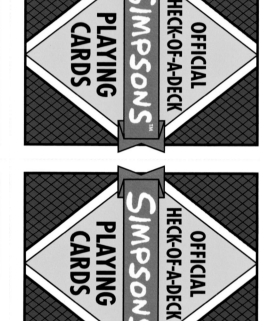

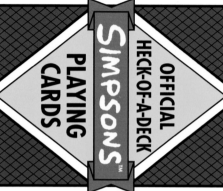

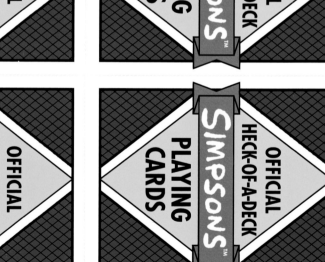

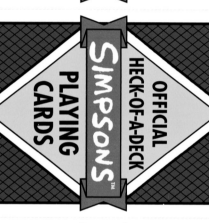

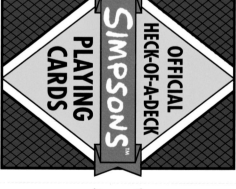

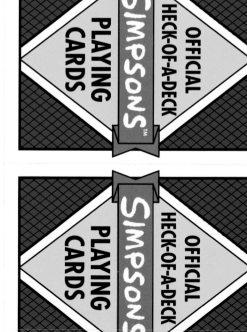

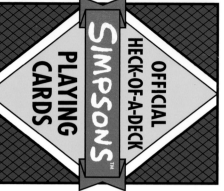

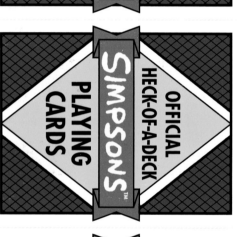

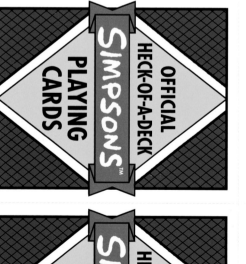

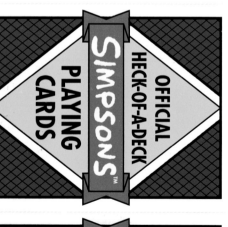

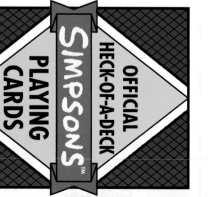

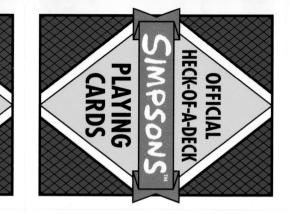

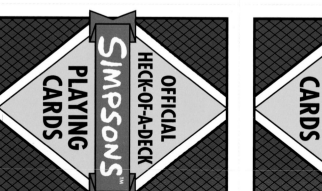

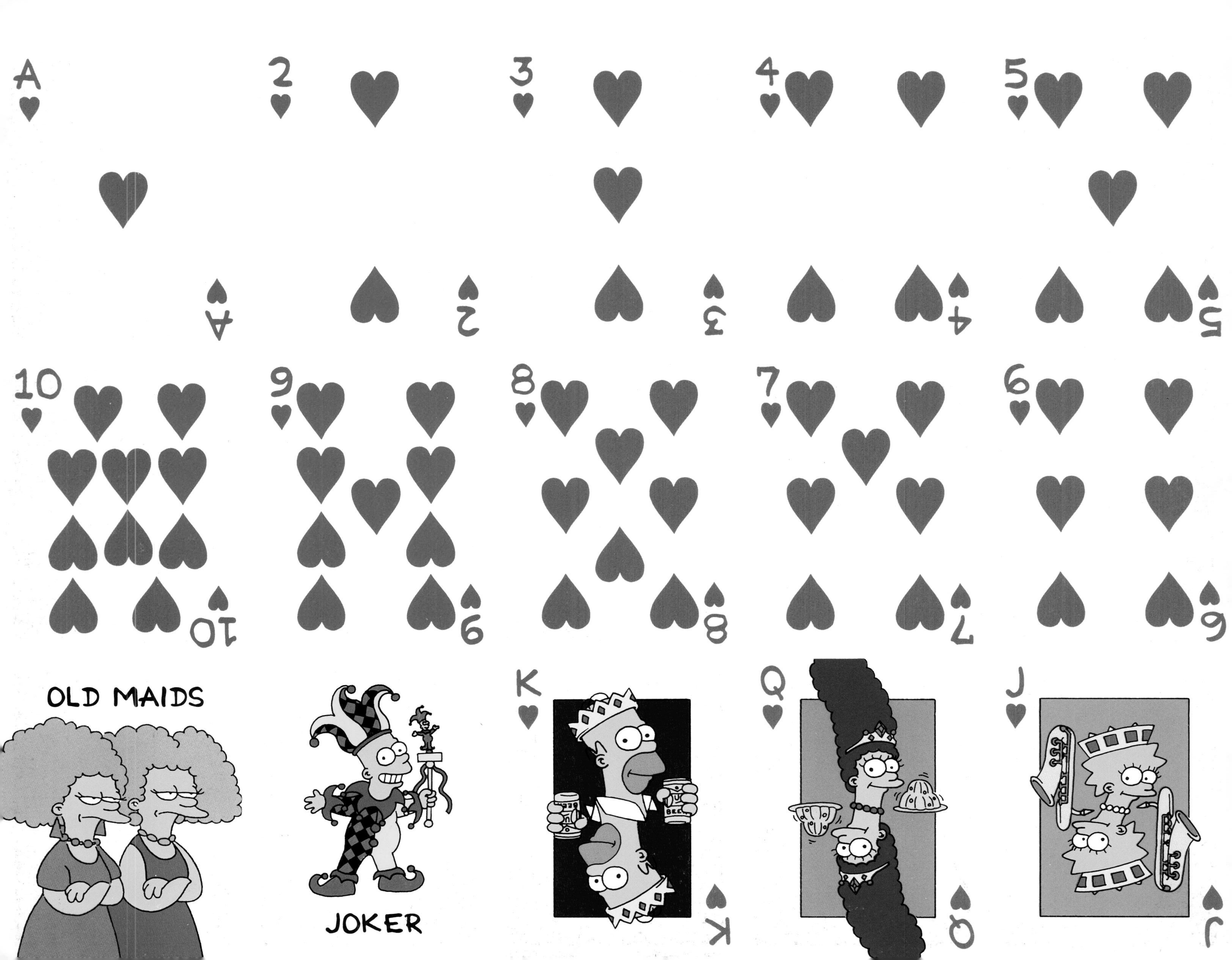
OLD MAIDS
JOKER

CUT ALONG BLUE LINES AND PLAY!

OFFICIAL
HECK-OF-A-DECK
SIMPSONS™
PLAYING
CARDS

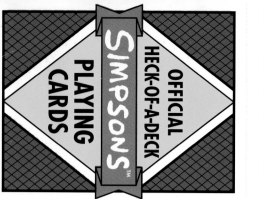

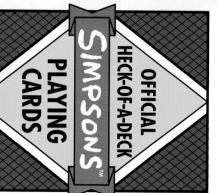

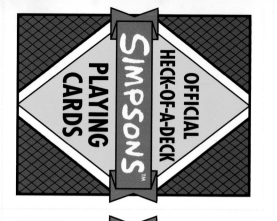

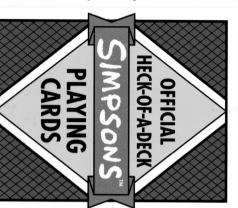

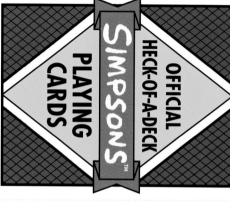

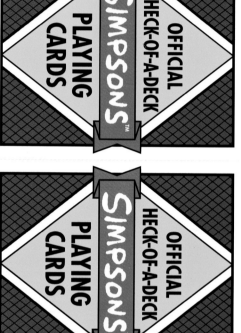

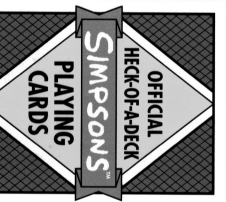

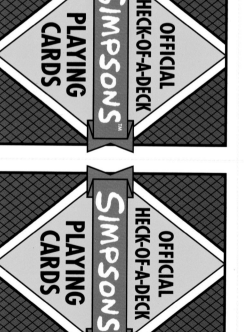

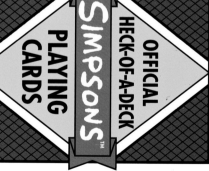

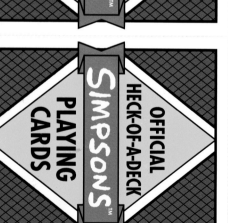

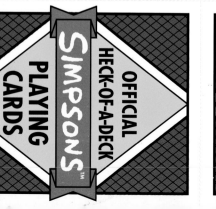

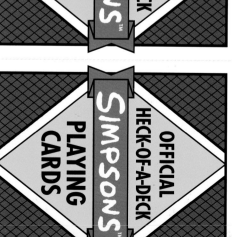

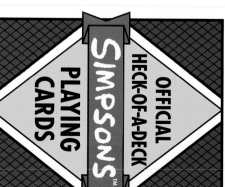

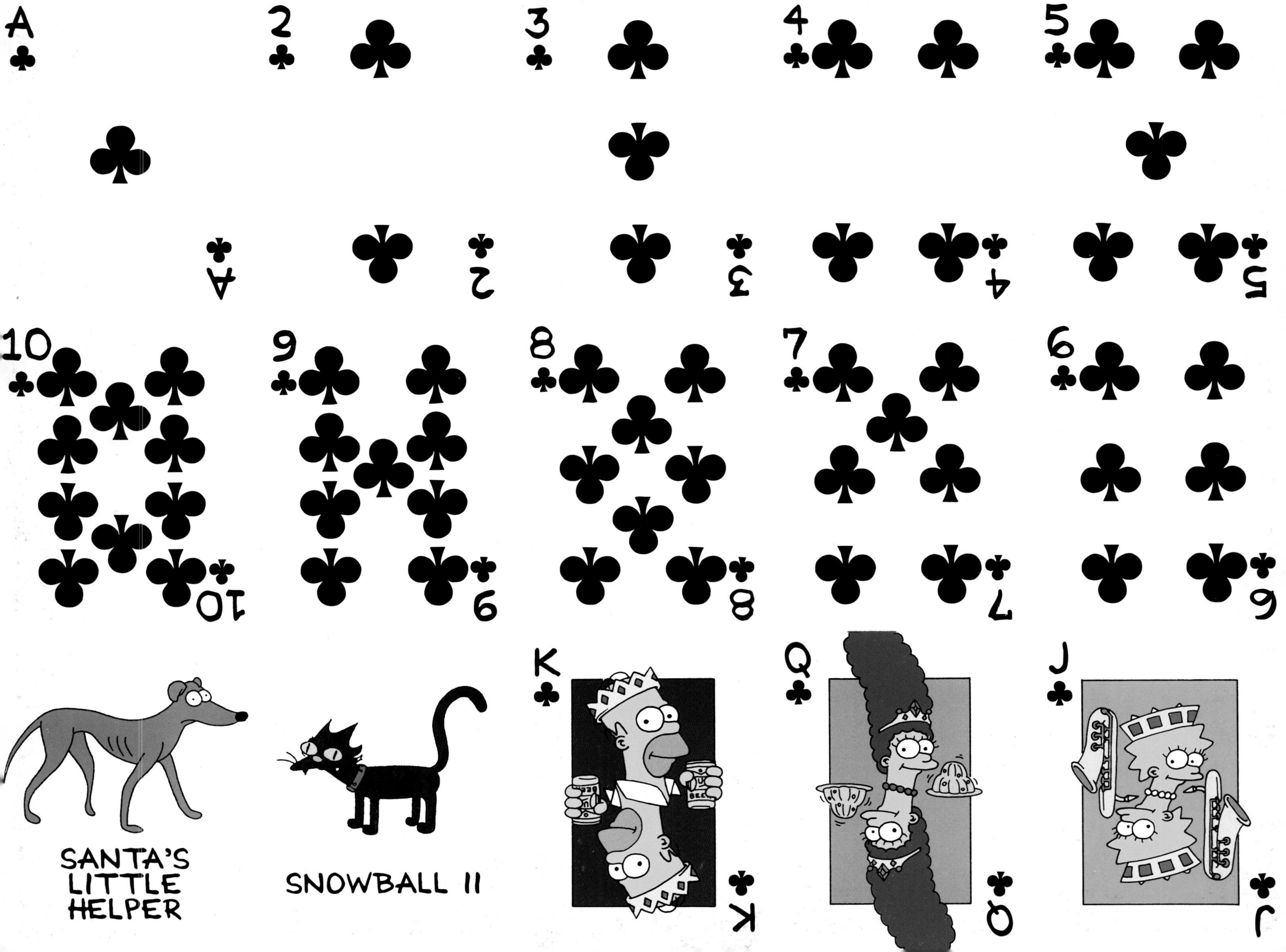
A
2
3
4
5
10
9
8
7
6
K
Q
J
SANTA'S LITTLE HELPER
SNOWBALL II

CUT ALONG BLUE LINES AND PLAY!

OFFICIAL
HECK-OF-A-DECK
SIMPSONS™
PLAYING
CARDS
OFFICIAL
HECK-OF-A-DECK
SIMPSONS™
PLAYING
CARDS
OFFICIAL
HECK-OF-A-DECK
SIMPSONS™
PLAYING
CARDS
OFFICIAL
HECK-OF-A-DECK
SIMPSONS™
PLAYING
CARDS
OFFICIAL
HECK-OF-A-DECK
SIMPSONS™
PLAYING
CARDS
OFFICIAL
HECK-OF-A-DECK
SIMPSONS™
PLAYING
CARDS
OFFICIAL
HECK-OF-A-DECK
SIMPSONS™
PLAYING
CARDS
OFFICIAL
HECK-OF-A-DECK
SIMPSONS™
PLAYING
CARDS
OFFICIAL
HECK-OF-A-DECK
SIMPSONS™
PLAYING
CARDS
OFFICIAL
HECK-OF-A-DECK
SIMPSONS™
PLAYING
CARDS
OFFICIAL
HECK-OF-A-DECK
SIMPSONS™
PLAYING
CARDS
OFFICIAL
HECK-OF-A-DECK
SIMPSONS™
PLAYING
CARDS
OFFICIAL
HECK-OF-A-DECK
SIMPSONS™
PLAYING
CARDS
OFFICIAL
HECK-OF-A-DECK
SIMPSONS™
PLAYING
CARDS
OFFICIAL
HECK-OF-A-DECK
SIMPSONS™
PLAYING
CARDS

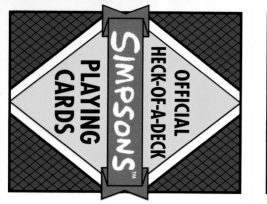

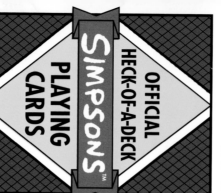

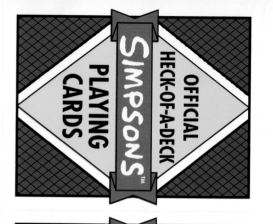

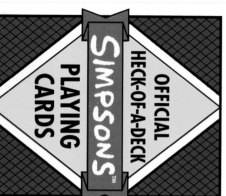

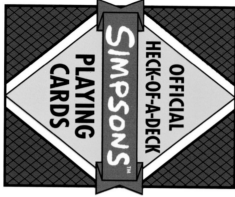

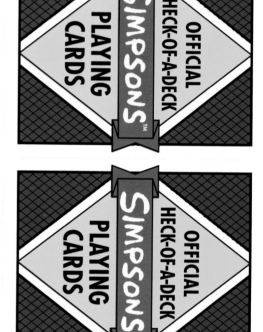

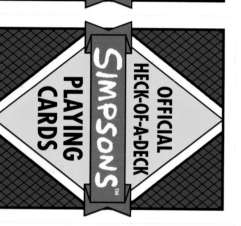

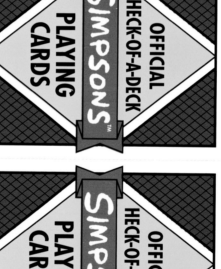

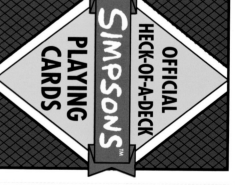

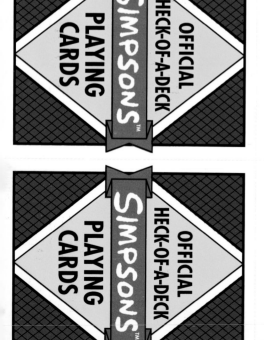

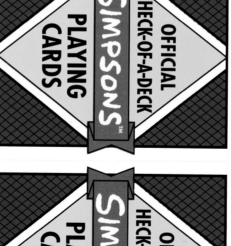

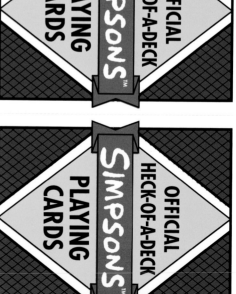

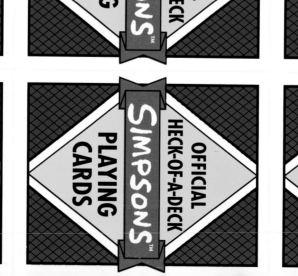

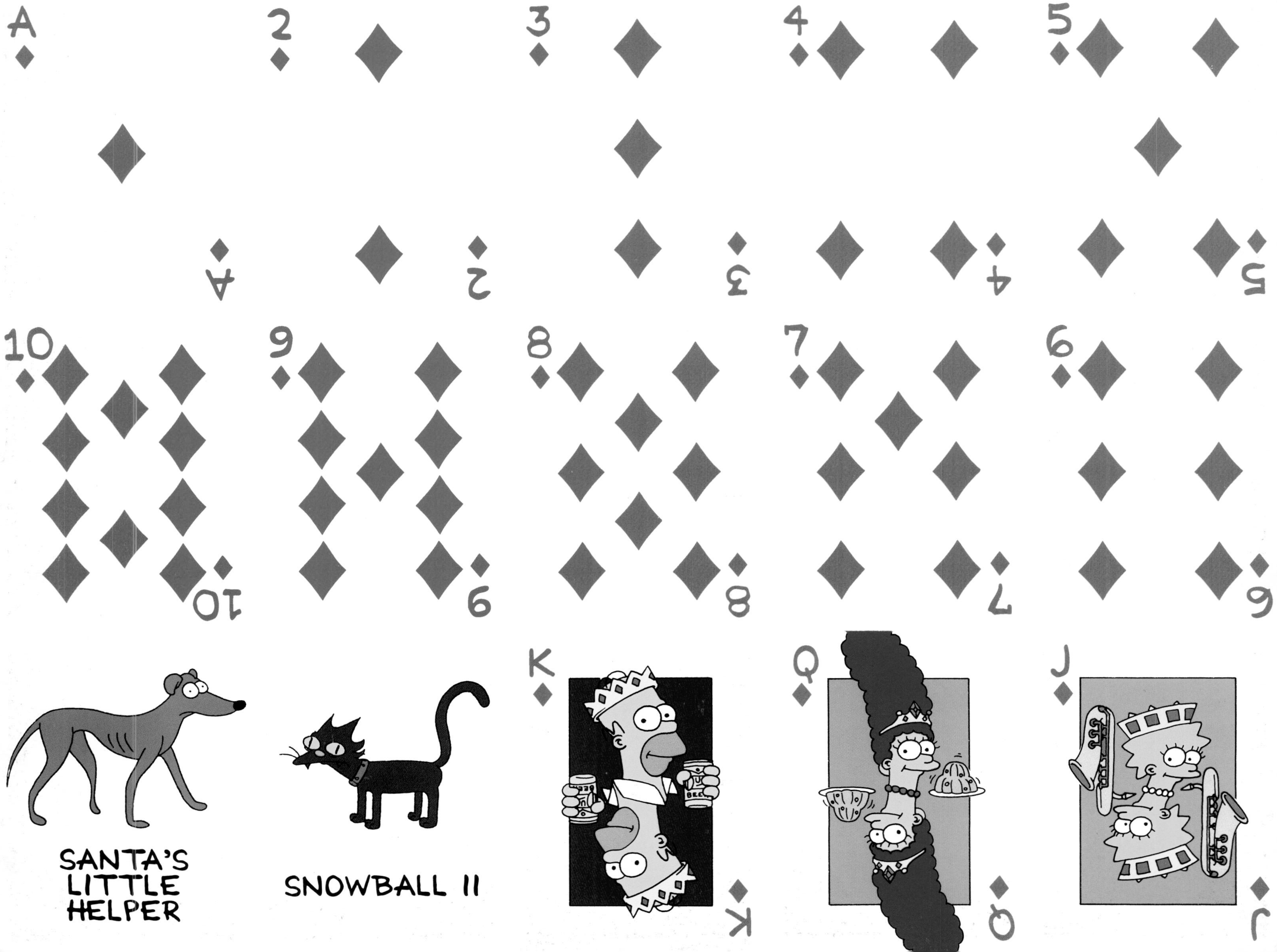
A
2
3
4
5
10
9
8
7
6
K
Q
J
SANTA'S LITTLE HELPER
SNOWBALL II

CUT ALONG BLUE LINES AND PLAY!

OFFICIAL
HECK-OF-A-DECK
SIMPSONS™
PLAYING
CARDS

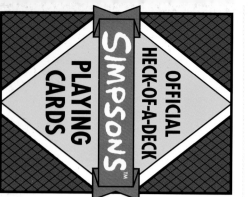

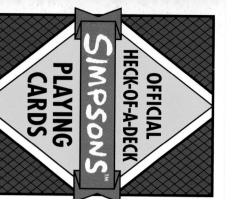

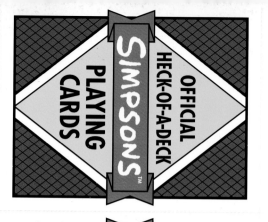

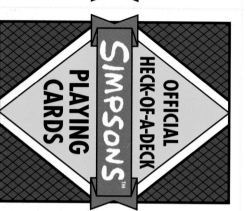

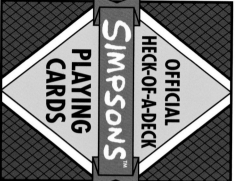

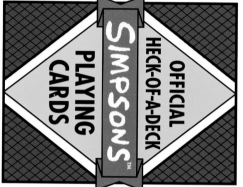

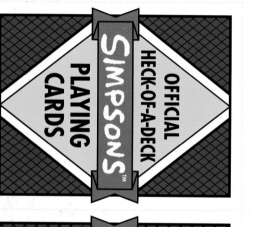

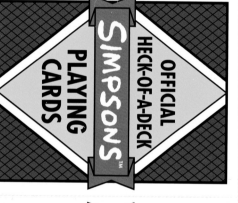

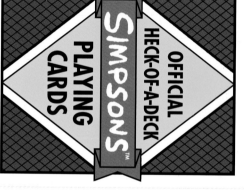

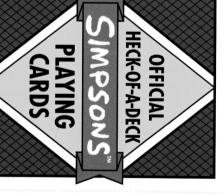

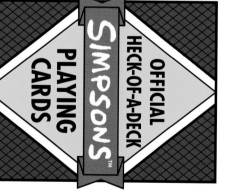

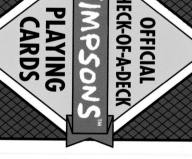

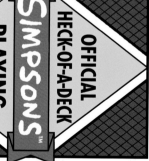

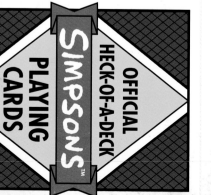

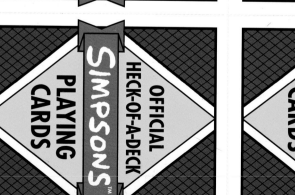

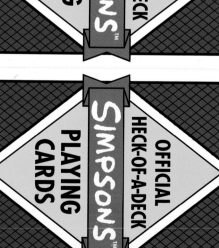

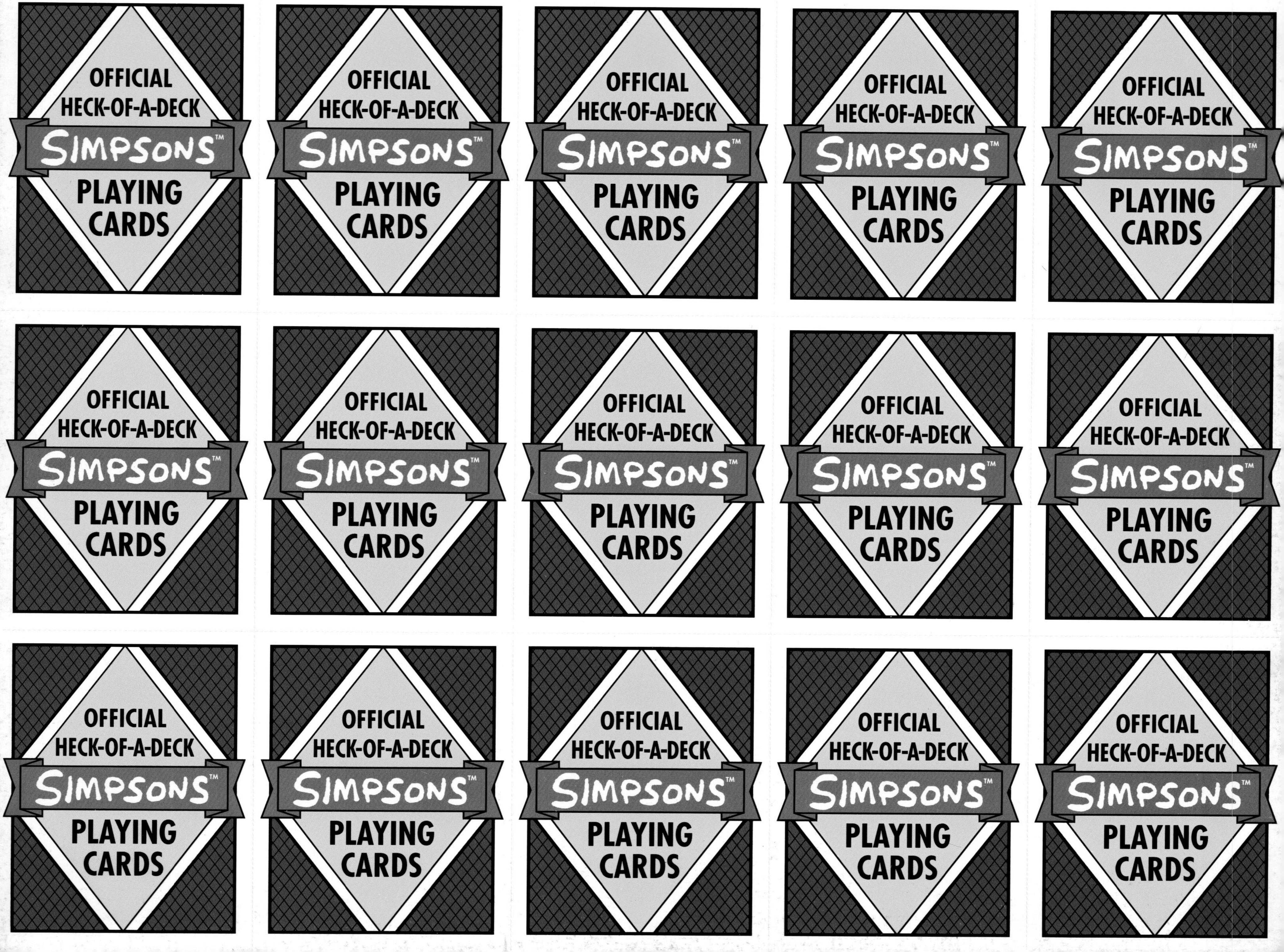

THE SIMPSONS'
HECK-OF-A-LOT MORE
CARD GAMES

PIG

For 3 to 13 players. Select as many four-of-a-kinds as there are players (for example, if you have four players, you'll use sixteen cards -- say, four Homers, four Marges, four Lisas and four fours). Shuffle and deal them out. Each player looks at his or her hand and then passes a card to the player on the left, and then another and another, the faster the better. As soon as anyone gets four-of-a-kind, he or she puts his or her finger on his nose and stops passing. As soon as you see someone do so, put your finger on your nose. The last one to do so loses. Appropriate pig sounds may be made at this (or any other) point in the game.

INDIAN HEAD POKER

Deal one card face-down to each player. At the count of three, everyone holds the card up to his or her forehead facing out. Starting with the player to the left of the dealer, bet on whether you think your card is the high card of the bunch. When the bets are all in put the cards on the table. High card wins.

PYRAMID

Lay 28 cards out in a pyramid, starting with one at the top, overlapping two beneath that, etc. The bottom row should have 7 cards. You remove any pair in the bottom row whose face value adds up to 13 and then any other such pair exposed as cards are removed (Jacks=11, Queens=12, Kings=13, Aces=1). The undealt cards are turned over one at a time, and can be used with whatever cards on the board are completely exposed. If you tear down the whole pyramid, you win.

RAIDING THE REFRIGERATOR

For 2 to 4 players. Deal everyone four cards, and place four cards face-up in the center--those are the midnight snacks. The rest of the cards are left face-down in one pile in the center, the pantry. You can steal food out of the fridge only if you have the matching card in your hand. Players go around in a circle, claiming their snacks by showing the card of the same rank from their hand, and placing their booty face-up in front of them. But watch out! If someone else has the same card too, he or she can swipe it from under your nose when it's his or her turn (you can't gorge yourself until the game is over). If it's your turn and you can't either raid the fridge or swipe a snack from someone else, you have to place one of your own cards face-up in the center. When everyone's hands (and stomachs) are empty, deal out four new helpings. Whoever ends up with his or her plate piled the highest wins.

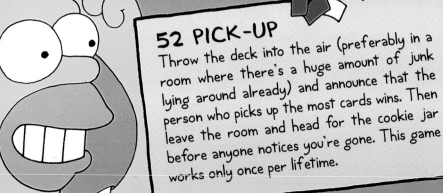

52 PICK-UP

Throw the deck into the air (preferably in a room where there's a huge amount of junk lying around already) and announce that the person who picks up the most cards wins. Then leave the room and head for the cookie jar before anyone notices you're gone. This game works only once per lifetime.

REVEALED AT LAST!
SOLUTIONS
TO OUR BAFFLING PUZZLES!

NO PEEKING, YOU TWO!

ANSWER: Lisa goes through the maze, but Bart cheats and gets there first.

GO NUTS FOR DONUTS

GET 'EM WHILE THEY'RE HOT 'N' DOUGHY

ANSWER: Everyone gets the donuts! Lisa gets through the maze, but of course she shares the donuts.

WHO IS IT?

MARGE   TEPEE

RABBIT   SAXOPHONE

SKATEBOARD   EARTH

HOMER   ICE CREAM

= SMITHERS

EYE TRICKS

1. A, B, C, D	3. NO
2. C	4. B
	5. B

MAGGIE'S MIXED-UP PICTURE SCRAMBLE

MARGE'S HAIRDO SECRET REBUSLY REVEALED

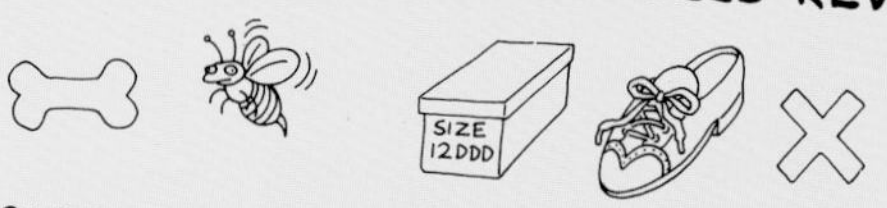

BONE - B + SHOEBOX - SHOE - X

+ B + BOY - O + PINEAPPLE - E - APPLE

ANSWER: ONE BOBBY PIN

PICNIC PANIC!

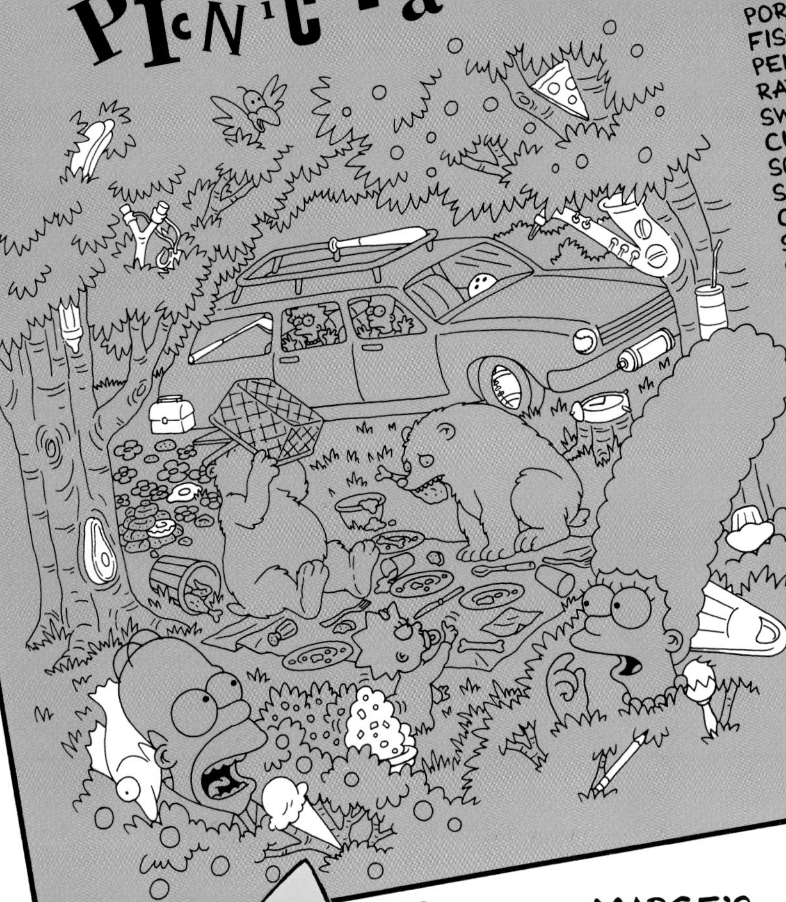

HOT DOG
SLINGSHOT
BABY BOTTLE
PORK CHOP
FISH
PENCIL
RATTLE
SWIM FIN
CUPCAKE
SODA CAN
SAXOPHONE
CLOCK
SPRAY CAN
SLICE OF PIZZA
BOWLING BALL
FOOTBALL
BASEBALL
GOLF CLUB
LUNCH PAIL
FRIED EGG
DONUT
ICE CREAM CONE
GELATIN DESSERT

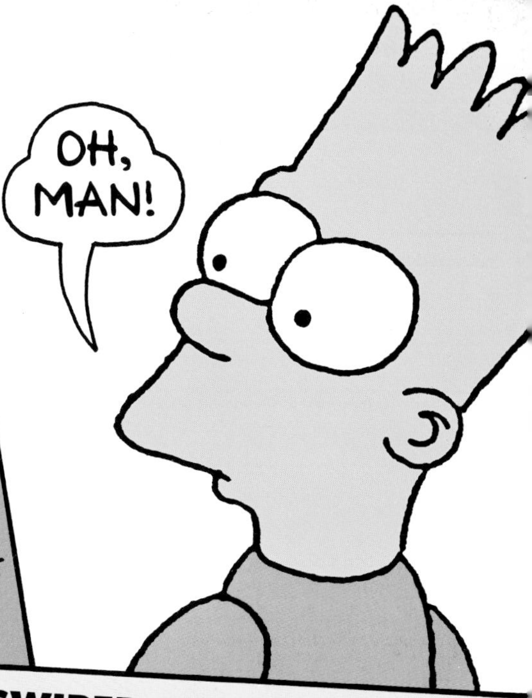
OH, MAN!

WHO SWIPED THE CUPCAKES?

ANSWER:

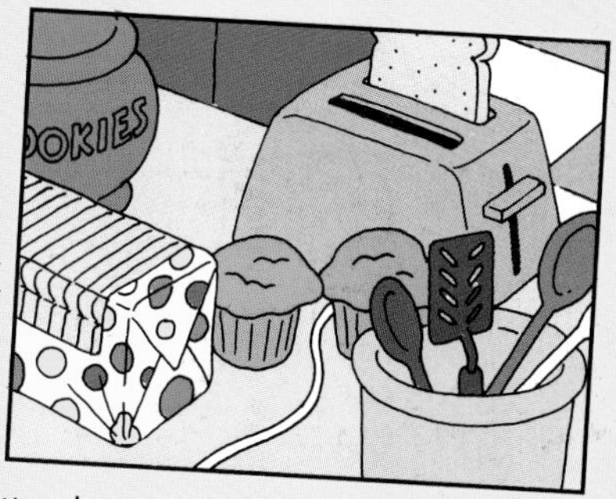
COOKIES

Maggie wanted the cupcakes, but couldn't reach them. Lisa was much too intent on her studies to even notice them. Bart looks guilty, but Bart always looks guilty. Snowball II looks suspicious enough, but since Marge's yummy cupcakes contain NO tuna or tuna by-products, she lacks motivation. Homer had the opportunity, the means and, knowing the cupcakes were intended for Patty and Selma, the motivation. It was Homer, all right. He stashed the cupcakes behind the toaster just as Marge left the kitchen and quickly turned his back on everyone else in the room.

MARGE'S WEEK-AT-A-GLANCE:
E, C, B, F, A, D

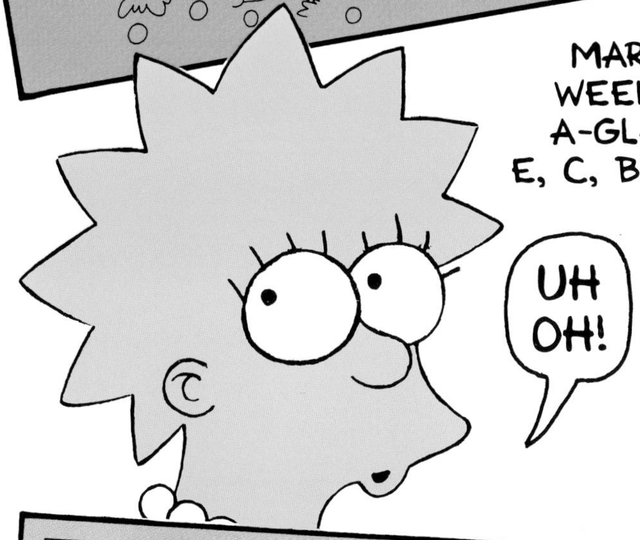
UH OH!

Otto's WILD RIDE!

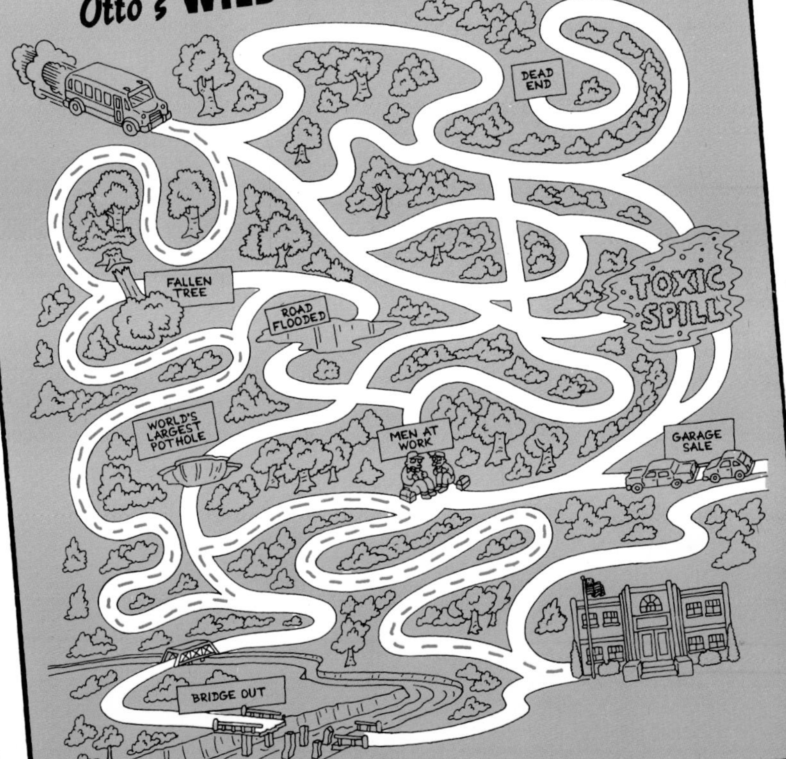
DEAD END
FALLEN TREE
ROAD FLOODED
TOXIC SPILL
WORLD'S LARGEST POTHOLE
MEN AT WORK
GARAGE SALE
BRIDGE OUT

1 I	2 M	■	3 B	4 A	5 R	6 T	■	7 S	8 I	9 M	10 P
11 S	12 O	13 N	■	14 W	15 H	16 O	■	17 T	18 H	19 E	■
20 H	21 E	22 L	23 L	■	24 A	25 R	26 E	■	27 y	28 O	29 U

DOUBLE ACROSTIC: ANSWER EACH OF THE QUESTIONS BELOW. THEN ENTER THE LETTERS INTO THE BOXES ABOVE ACCORDING TO THE NUMBERS INDICATED.

A. Word before dog or foot or rod. H (15) O (12) T (6)

B. Weak; spineless. W (14) I (1) M (9) P (10) y (27)

C. Head of the House of Simpson. H (20) O (16) M (2) E (26) R (5)

D. What Bart is to the above. S (7) O (28) N (13)

E. John or Paul or George or Ringo. B (3) E (19) A (24) T (17) L (23) E (21)

F. Ben's last name. H (18) U (29) R (25)

G. Simpson sibling. L (22) I (8) S (11) A (4)

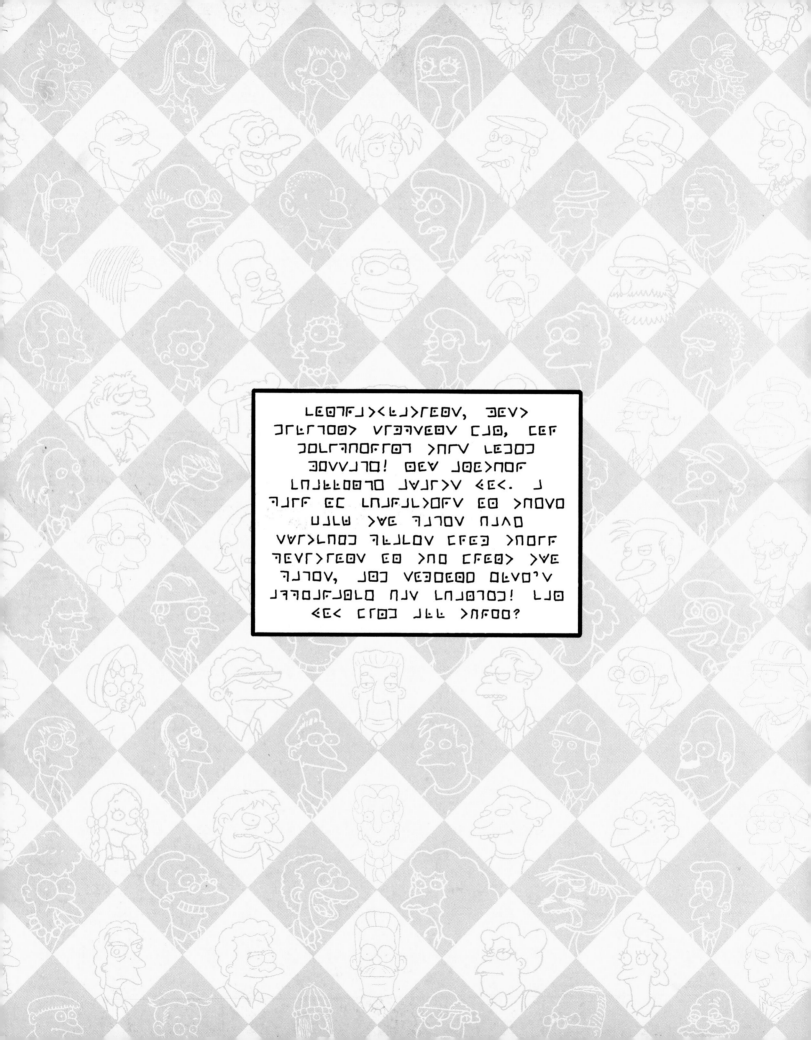